the lost majority

the lost majority

The 2017 election, the Conservative Party,
the voters and the future

Michael A. Ashcroft

@LordAshcroft

Biteback Publishing

First published in Great Britain in 2017 by
Biteback Publishing Ltd
Westminster Tower
3 Albert Embankment
London SE1 7SP
Copyright © Michael A. Ashcroft 2017

ISBN 978-1-78590-333-5

10 9 8 7 6 5 4 3 2 1

A CIP catalogue record for this book is available from the British Library.

Set in Adobe Garamond Pro

Printed and bound in Great Britain by
CPI Group (UK) Ltd, Croydon CR0 4YY

Contents

About the author

LORD ASHCROFT KCMG PC is an international businessman, author, philanthropist and pollster. From 2005 to 2010 he was deputy chairman of the Conservative Party, having been its Treasurer from 1998 to 2001. He the founder and chairman of the board of Crimestoppers, a trustee of the Imperial War Museum, chairman of the trustees of Ashcroft Technology Academy, Chancellor of Anglia Ruskin University and Treasurer of the International Democrat Union. In September 2012 he was appointed the Prime Minister's Special Representative on Veterans' Transition.

Lord Ashcroft's political works include *Smell the Coffee: A Wake-Up Call for the Conservative Party*; *Minority Verdict: The Conservative Party, the Voters and the 2010 Election*; *Pay Me Forty Quid and I'll Tell You: The 2015 Election through the Eyes of the Voters* and *Well, You Did Ask: Why the UK Voted to Leave the EU* (both with Kevin Culwick); *Call Me Dave: The Unauthorised Biography of David Cameron* (with Isabel Oakeshott); and *Hopes and Fears: Trump, Clinton, the Voters and the Future*. His other works include *Victoria Cross Heroes*; *Special Forces Heroes*; *George Cross Heroes*; *Heroes of the Skies*; *Special Ops Heroes* and *Victoria Cross Heroes II*.

His political research and commentary is published at LordAshcroftPolls.com. For more information about Lord Ashcroft visit LordAshcroft.com. You can also follow him on Twitter: @LordAshcroft.

www.lordashcroftpolls.com | www.lordashcroft.com | @LordAshcroft

Introduction: Time to smell the coffee all over again

IF, THE DAY AFTER THE 2015 ELECTION, you had told the Tories that the next time round they could have 42 per cent of the vote – take it or leave it – they would have taken it. In fact, they would have bitten your arm off. It would mean that even after presiding over seven years of austerity, the Conservative Party would increase its support in three consecutive elections, twice in government, and receive its highest vote share since 1983.

That is what happened in June 2017, and it was an amazing political achievement. But the Conservatives had not bargained for Labour being just two points, or fewer than 800,000 votes, behind them. Rather than the thumping outright victory that history might have led them to expect from such a vote share, the working majority the Tories had unexpectedly won 25 months earlier was thrown away in unnecessary exchange for a hung parliament. Theresa May's decision to hold a snap election two years into a five-year term (the only two years of undiluted Conservative government in the previous twenty) was, on that score, a giant miscalculation.

I want to help understand how this extraordinary result came about. In this book, and through the research it brings together, I will explore what the election tells us about the state of politics in Britain and the implications for the future, especially for the Conservative Party.

Some of the reasons for the unexpected outcome are easy to see, at least in retrospect. For one thing, people do not like unnecessary elections, especially if they are already weary from three years of relentless campaigning – the referendums on Scottish independence and European Union membership, either side of a still recent general election, had amounted to what felt like an age of uninterrupted politics. This goes double if they think the election in question is being held for party advantage. Many people did not accept Mrs. May's explanation that the national interest compelled her to seek a clear mandate to negotiate Britain's EU exit, seeing instead a transparent attempt to boost her power base. As the BBC's Nick Robinson asked the Prime Minister the morning after she announced the contest: "What is it about the 20-point opinion poll lead that first attracted you to the idea of an early election?"

For another thing, you cannot tell the voters what an election is about. Instruct them to vote on one thing – securing strong and stable leadership and strengthening the PM's hand in Brexit negotiations, for example – and some of them might be contrary enough to vote on something else altogether, like austerity, pensions or the NHS.

The Conservatives' biggest mistake was to overestimate the extent to which Brexit would play to their advantage. Relatively few voters thought both that the EU negotiations were among the most important issues facing the country (let alone themselves and their families) and that the Conservatives were the best party to handle them. More specifically, previous Labour supporters who had voted to leave the EU proved less willing to back Theresa May than the Tories had hoped. One reason was that for many, their referendum votes had been a reaction to feeling perpetually overlooked in political debate, weariness with austerity, and concerns about public services. Jeremy

Corbyn, then, was right up their street. To add to this, suspicion of the Conservatives in Labour heartlands proved persistent and widespread. For too many, including pro-Brexit Labour voters, the idea of putting their cross next to the name of the Tory candidate remained unthinkable, and waverers were reminded – not least through a brilliantly orchestrated social media campaign to highlight emotive subjects like fox hunting – that the Conservative Party was not for people like them.

At the same time, the Tories did not reckon with the reaction to Brexit among existing Conservatives who had voted to remain in the EU. Nearly half of the younger members of this group (that is, those aged under 50; we are talking about the Tories, remember) did not vote for the party at this election. Our analysis shows that differences with the party over Britain's EU departure were the most important motivation for Conservative "defectors" – which helps explain how the Tories came to lose such remain-voting seats as Twickenham, Kingston & Surbiton and Oxford West & Abingdon.

Those who did not see Brexit as the overriding issue of the day found precious little else in the Conservative manifesto to stir their interest. Removing the triple lock on pensions, reforming social care funding, means-testing the Winter Fuel Payment and ending universal free school meals for infants may all have been defensible enough – tough decisions on difficult issues as part of a balanced plan for government. But as far as many voters were concerned, that was all there was. Nothing came across to follow through on Theresa May's pledge on taking office to govern for those who were "just about managing", to spread opportunity, to give them more control over their lives and ensure prosperity was shared. There was no visible equivalent of the Help to Buy scheme that showed many young people in 2015 that the Tories understood their aspirations – in that case, to own their own home – and wanted to help fulfil them. This time, the Conservative programme seemed unrelentingly grim: as one man told us after the election, having considered the

Tories but decided against, "I always did believe in economics and not spending what you don't have, but I'm fed up with being shafted so I voted Labour."

None of this was helped by what voters regarded as an uninspiring and rather complacent Conservative campaign. The decision for Theresa May not to take part in head-to-head television debates was probably right. I have written before about the distraction they can be in a campaign, with the leader and senior staff spending long hours on "debate prep" that would be better employed on more fruitful activity, and how the focus on two or three such events can detract from a party's wider message. But the explanation that the PM is skipping TV shows in order to meet real voters only really works if that is what she is actually doing. Time and again in our research people would comment on the difference between Mrs. May's closed meetings with Tory activists and Jeremy Corbyn's appearances in more public settings. She is evidently less comfortable on the campaign trail than her predecessor, but this safety-first approach only added to the impression that the Conservatives thought they had it in the bag from the outset and need only go through the motions. It also prompted some to think that the Tories didn't offer any more enticing policy ideas because they didn't think they needed to.

On top of all that, the appeal of Jeremy Corbyn's Labour Party turned out to be greater than anyone imagined, including Labour itself. After I suggested early in the campaign that the party could end up with as few as 160 seats, more than one Labour MP contacted me privately to say this sounded wrong – it was going to be much worse for them than that. (In the event, they won 262.) Soon after the election was called, many lifelong Labour voters in my focus groups complained that Corbyn was hopeless and his party was a shambles. But as the days and weeks went by, and they saw him out and about with real people and liberated from his internal party scrapping, more and more people began to warm to him. They saw that he had withstood a fearsome battering from the media and his opponents, and had done so with remarkable resilience and good grace. Whether or not they could see him at Number Ten, many came to see him as principled and well-intentioned, not the dangerous menace they had been told about. Labour put forward policies that people believed would improve their lives, and managed to project an overall message of optimism and hope: as more than one person told us in our post-election research in a presumably unconscious echo of Donald Trump, Jeremy Corbyn wanted to "make Britain great again".

There is a comforting theory that large numbers of people voted Labour safe in the knowledge that they would still have a Tory government afterwards, but there is little evidence to support it in the research assembled here. After the election, I found Labour voters were happier with their decision than Tories. And while most people expected a Conservative victory, vanishingly few of those who did not vote Tory said they would do so if they had the chance to go back and vote again.

*   *   *

Twelve years ago, after the Tories lost their third election in a row, I published a detailed study of public opinion titled *Smell the Coffee: A Wake-Up Call for the Conservative Party*. I did not pull my punches, concluding that the reason the Tories kept losing "was not that millions of people in Britain thought the Conservative Party wasn't like them and didn't understand them; the problem was that they were right." It would be something of an exaggeration to claim the Tories are in the same predicament after the 2017 election as they were after winning just 32 per cent of the vote and 198 parliamentary seats. But it is no less important to learn from what happened, and to take stock of the party's relationship with the voters – especially those who came to the Conservatives for the first time, those whose support it lost, those it thought it would win over but didn't, and those who were inspired to cast their first ever ballot, or their first for a long time, for someone else. That is what I have tried to do in the chapters that follow. The extensive research I have described in them explores how people reacted to the campaigns, why people ended up voting as they did, how they see the parties' priorities in relation to their own, the effect of Brexit on their voting decisions, the outlook of younger voters, and how they see things in the light of the result, among many other things. The findings speak for themselves, but they lead me to two fundamental observations.

The first, as in 2005, is about the Conservative brand. At their best, the Tories have shown themselves to be a party of freedom, responsibility, aspiration and opportunity, wanting to help people make the best of life and working to spread prosperity and success. In their recent victories, though, they have been seen as a party that might not be very nice but at least knew what it was doing – or was at least more capable of running things than its opponents. Many voted Conservative not because of any affinity with the party, or because they thought the Tories had their interests at heart, but to get the job done. But despite more than a decade of "modernisation", in the aftermath of the 2017 debacle voters find the Conservative Party no more sympathetic to their aspirations and anxieties than they did before but, crucially, no more competent than it is sympathetic. And if Labour look no more proficient than the Tories, they seem to many people to have just as much of a vision for the country, and a rather more uplifting one at that. In the space of a few weeks, the Conservatives lost their crucial competitive advantage. With many people anxious about how the country will emerge from a time of real uncertainty, the Tories have to restore confidence quickly. Then they must give people a more compelling reason to want them in government than being less likely than Labour to foul up the running of a whelk stall.

The second is that talk of the lost majority doesn't just apply to the Conservatives. The question now is where any party finds a majority in parliament if 42 per cent of the vote and 13,669,883 individual ballots in your favour is not enough to get you one. The key is in building coalitions. The Conservative voting coalition in 2017 was bigger than it was two years earlier, but it was also different: older, more working class, more modestly educated, more socially and culturally conservative, and more pro-Brexit. In some ways this represents a real achievement, especially when considered in terms of geography: a few years ago it was just not on the cards that we would soon see Tory MPs in Stoke, Mansfield, Middlesbrough and Walsall.

But in the face of the divisions that were exposed by the EU referendum, the challenge for political leaders has been to hold together supporters of different backgrounds and viewpoints as much as to add to them. Yet those who switched away from the Conservatives at this election were younger, more likely to be graduates and professionals, and more socially liberal – people who constitute a growing part of the electorate – than those who stayed or joined. They were also more likely to have voted to remain in the EU, along with nearly half the country. A party that aspires to govern for the whole United Kingdom will have to be able to appeal more widely beyond the dividing lines of remain or leave.

On the day she took office, Theresa May was onto something when she talked in Downing Street about leading one nation and building a country that works for everyone. Somewhere along the way, that message has become blurred. As we know from the Conservative Party's long struggle to show wary voters that it had changed, in the absence of persuasive new evidence people quickly fall back on their old assumptions. It's time to smell the coffee all over again.

1 / **The modernising years**

TWO SHORT YEARS AGO, in the appendix to *Call Me Dave*, my unauthorised biography of the then Prime Minister, I looked back at the coalition government and the 2015 election. The section examining Tories and their first outright victory for 23 years was titled *The Conservatives: Job Done?* The job in question was that of transforming the view of the Conservative Party that prevailed from the mid-1990s to its third consecutive election defeat in May 2005.

The party's problem was its brand. Everything a political party does is seen through the prism of what people already think of it: its character, its motives, its competence, whose side it seems to be on. New policies, I argued in *Smell the Coffee*, my review of that election, would not be enough: "The brand problem means that the most robust, coherent, principled and attractive Conservative policies will have no impact on the voters who mistrust our motivation and doubt our ability to deliver." And while proper targeting was important and sophisticated campaign techniques could be effective, they essentially helped maximise a party's performance given the circumstances: it was the big picture that really counted.

I have now been studying that big picture for twelve years. At that stage, it was not a pretty one. The Conservative Party's average poll rating in January 1993 was 39 per cent. A year later it was 31 per cent, and there it stayed, or within the margin of error, every January for eleven years. At the time of my research in the months leading up to Tony

Blair's third victory, the Tories were widely regarded as being stuck in the past – which may not be unrelated to the fact that two thirds of Conservative supporters thought Britain had been a better place to live in twenty or thirty years earlier. Some thought that if the Tories had a virtue it was that they were patriotic, but in an old-fashioned sort of way that harked back to the good old days and how things used to be. Most people did not think the Conservatives shared their values, cared about ordinary people or were likely to deliver what they promised, but neither did they think the party was competent and capable – a fatal combination of flaws. The party that had once been associated with aspiration and opportunity seemed to many to be out of touch and to care most about the interests of the well-off. Despite having had eight years in opposition to ponder the problem, the Conservative Party seemed no different from the one that had been booted out of office with such relish in 1997.

My daily tracking research during the 2005 election campaign found that only two Conservative messages cut through to the public. One was a promise to cut taxes, which most people did not believe. The other was a pledge to reduce immigration, an issue on which the Tories already had a huge lead. The party did not come close to challenging the Labour government on managing the economy or improving public services, both of which mattered more to most voters. The Conservative Party's campaign slogan in 2005 was "Are you thinking what we're thinking?", but the answer was "No".

*   *   *

Five years later, David Cameron walked into 10 Downing Street as the new Conservative Prime Minister. This was in many ways a remarkable feat: the Tories had never before managed to return to government from a position as weak as the one they faced going into the 2010 election. For outright victory, the Tories needed to pick up seats and shift the popular vote on a scale seen only once since the Second World War, in the New Labour landslide of 1997. Not only that, they would have to do it with constituency boundaries which heavily favoured their opponents. In the event, they gained 96 seats, their best performance since 1931 (which, with a National Government and a Labour schism, was such an unusual year that 2010 was arguably the best Conservative election result ever).

But the Tories were disappointed. They had faced a tired and chaotic government headed by a hapless and unpopular Prime Minister, and which had presided over a recession, a financial crisis and a huge public deficit. Shortly before polling day more than eight in ten voters were saying it was time for change, yet only 36 per cent ended up voting Conservative. The party was back in government, but with no majority of its own. The question Tories were asking was not "How did we do so well?" but "How did we do so badly that we've ended up having to govern in coalition with the Liberal Democrats?"

David Cameron had made it his mission to transform the Conservative Party. At the launch of his 2005 leadership campaign he reminded his audience that voters at the recent election had had no particular fondness for Labour: "The problem was that people didn't yet trust the Conservative Party, and it's we who've got to change." The party would need to "think, look and feel and sound like a completely different organisation". On his first day in the job he set out his aim that the Conservative Party should become "a voice for hope, optimism and change", and embarked on a series of initiatives designed to underline the point, some of which were greeted with dismay from elements within the party unconvinced by its new direction.

Cameron launched policy reviews on such un-Tory-sounding themes as social justice, global poverty, quality of life and public services, as well as more familiar areas of economic competitiveness and national security. He ordered a revamp of the selection process for prospective MPs, with the aim of recruiting more female and ethnic minority candidates. He tried to challenge the idea that the Tories were in the pockets of big business by criticising companies he felt had behaved badly, and campaigned heavily on the environment: his husky-accompanied trip to a Norwegian glacier to highlight his concern over climate change came to symbolise the new leader's modernisation project.

The voters noticed all this activity; they just weren't sure what to make of it. People could see that the youthful and energetic Cameron was a different kind of Tory leader from what they were used to, and seemed to have a different agenda. Whether the Conservative Party itself had changed, or was changing, was another question altogether. The research I conducted for the party in my capacity as Deputy Chairman began to find people wondering what the Tories really stood for, whether apparent changes were real or cosmetic, and whether the party was looking seriously at new areas or simply jumping on passing bandwagons. It also underlined that momentum had to be permanent. In the absence of a constant stream of new evidence, people would quickly fall back on their old impressions: asked in our regular "brand tracker" focus groups to choose from a large selection of images the ones that best represented the Tories, participants would nearly always seize on the picture of a posh-looking family standing outside an enormous house. Even so, people sensed that there was life in Cameron's Conservative Party, and by the middle of 2006 it had established its first consistent poll lead for thirteen years.

It lasted fourteen months. The Tory advance had been helped by a weary Labour government, widely felt not to have delivered on its promises, believed to favour those who did nothing to help themselves over hard-working people who tried to do the right thing, and worn down by lingering anger over its role in the Iraq war, not to mention the interminable saga over who would succeed Tony Blair and when, which made the party seem divided and self-indulgent. In June 2007, all that seemed to change. Gordon Brown's accession to the premiership brought about a surge in Labour's fortunes, or at least its poll ratings, which seemed to the Tories as though it was never going to end. If the new PM was dour and rumpled, at least he was a refreshing change from the slickness and tarnished dazzle of the Blair years. Indeed, "change" was Gordon Brown's mantra in his early days at Number Ten. Some voters were unsure what new ideas and policies this change would entail, or indeed what he had been doing at the top of government for the last decade if he thought so much about it needed changing, but were more than prepared to give him the benefit of the doubt.

As well as having to watch their new opponent in his ascendancy, the Tories suffered their own mishaps, including a noisy internal row about grammar schools and an ill-fated trip by David Cameron to Rwanda, where he was asked by a local TV reporter if he ought not to be at home attending to the flooding in his Witney constituency. While the Conservative Party struggled to articulate a message, Britain saw the first signs of the financial crisis, as the government stepped in to guarantee deposits at the Northern Rock bank. This only strengthened Mr. Brown: if the country was facing turbulent economic times, who better to be in charge than the erstwhile Iron Chancellor?

With all the political indicators in Labour's favour, expectations grew that the Prime Minister would try to turn his extended honeymoon into a new mandate and call a general election. Indeed, the question dominated politics for weeks on end, with Cabinet ministers openly pondering the pros and cons of going to the country ("it's an interesting question as to where the gamble really lies", as Ed Balls put it on the *Today* programme in September).

Whether Mr. Brown would have won an early election is a question that can never be answered. What is certain is that his decision not to hold one transformed his reputation: one week he was strong and decisive, the next, weak and dithering. Worse, he insisted that the tightening polls in the days before the announcement – which had followed an eye-catching Tory conference in which George Osborne had pledged to raise the Inheritance Tax threshold to £1 million, and David Cameron had delivered a rousing unscripted closing speech concluding with a challenge to Brown to "go ahead and call that election" – had had nothing to do with his decision. That sounded so unlikely as to do away with the idea that he was more honest and straightforward than your average politician. Voters had given him the benefit of the doubt; now they wondered if he was up to the job.

From that point on, David Cameron topped the polls as the best available Prime Minister, and Labour's economic problems were only just beginning. As the credit crunch took hold, the government was forced to nationalise Northern Rock. Confidence in the administration was undermined by a series of blunders, including the revelation that HM Revenue & Customs had contrived to lose the bank details of 25 million individuals. People complained more and more loudly about the rising cost of living. At the height of the financial crisis in 2008 the government announced a £400 billion rescue package for British banks. In January 2009 came the news that the country was officially in recession. Three months later the Chancellor, Alistair Darling, announced a record budget deficit of £175 billion.

Labour tried to turn these troubling times to their political advantage. Gordon Brown played a prominent role in international efforts to tackle the crisis, and argued at home that now was "no time for a novice". But our research at the time found that the bigger question about the opposition in voters' minds was not their lack of experience, but quite how a Conservative government would be different or better. Rather than explain this, the Tories' priority seemed to be to argue ceaselessly that the crisis was all Gordon Brown's fault. Undecided voters were not convinced that this was the case: people were more likely to blame the banks or global markets than the PM. More to the point, they were more interested in how to get out of the mess than in who had caused it, and as far as they could tell, the Tories did not have much in the way of an alternative plan.

One exception to this was the deficit, which the Shadow Chancellor, George Osborne, had made clear would be his priority at the Treasury. In his final conference speech before the election he bravely set out some of his plans, including freezing public sector pay, restricting tax credits, and bringing forward the date at which the retirement age would rise. But achieving his aim of balancing the books would mean extending austerity much further. Mr. Osborne vowed to protect spending on the NHS and international development, but beyond that, there was not a great deal of reassurance he could offer. There would be cuts, and not just cuts but "Tory cuts". If the Conservatives had the ruthless streak needed to get to grips with the public finances, there were fears that this was the kind of job they would set about with a bit too much relish: swing voters in particular worried that the Tories would cut in ways that would damage public services and harm ordinary people.

Doubts about the Conservative Party's motives and priorities, in other words, had not yet been put to rest. The Tories' relentless assault on Gordon Brown came at the cost of missing the chance to set out a clear alternative and demonstrate their good intentions to those who doubted them. This meant that Labour scaremongering about Tory plans gained more traction than they would otherwise have done; even for people who had had more than enough of Labour, the decision to switch to the Conservatives became much harder than it might have been. Moreover, if the Brown bashing had been intended to clarify the choice, it had the opposite effect, reinforcing the view that the parties were much the same. This created an opening for the Liberal Democrat leader, Nick Clegg, in what was for many voters his revelatory performance in the televised debates: if Labour and the Tories represented the same old politics, here was another way of voting for change.

By election day in 2010, too few were persuaded that the change they wanted and the change the Tories were offering were the same thing. Even after five years of David Cameron, not enough voters had been reassured that the Conservative Party itself had changed, and was now on their side.

* * *

But at least it was in government. After 13 years of only being able to talk, the Tories now had a chance to complete, through their actions in office, the rehabilitation of the Conservative brand. By keeping their promises and showing that they could govern in the interests of everyone, they would have the chance to dispel their caricature as a party for the privileged few.

This would be easier said than done given that there was, in the now immortal words of the note left by the outgoing Chief Secretary to the Treasury for his successor, "no money". From the moment the coalition set about tackling the deficit, they faced complaints that they were cutting "too far and too fast". At the same time, however, people would concede that the alternative was to cut less and more slowly, which meant borrowing more for longer, which sounded like a dangerous mistake. If voters did not find austerity especially palatable, they gave David Cameron's government credit for getting to grips with the job in hand. Throughout the parliament, my research found that the attribute with which they were most associated, and the one on which they had the biggest lead over Labour, was being willing to take tough decisions for the long term.

The air of competence that the Tories had painstakingly established took a beating in 2012 after the so-called "Omnishambles" Budget, a series of high-profile policy U-turns and a row about a minor adjustment to the VAT treatment of baked goods that became known as the "pasty tax". The decision to cut the top rate of income tax from 50 to 45 per cent on incomes over £150,000 was also controversial, confirming to some that the Tories were more interested in helping those who had already made it than in making life easier for those who were struggling to get by. The Conservatives tried to reassert their claim to be the party of the strivers: David Cameron adopted the theme that Britain was in a "global race" and said he wanted to build an "aspiration nation"; the Tories were not the party of the better off, he told his conference that autumn, but "the party of the want-to-be better off, those who strive to make a better life for themselves and their families".

There was praise for the government's reforms to the welfare system, and particularly the changes to ensure that people were always better off in work than they would be on benefits. Many also strongly approved of the Conservatives' immigration policy, creating a new Border Force and aiming to reduce overall annual net migration to less than 100,000, but they were much less clear that these intentions were being put into practice (the immigration target was ultimately missed by some distance; the final figures before the 2015 election put net migration at 298,000). The Tories also suffered a setback, arguably self-inflicted, over the National Health Service, an issue that regularly tops voters' priority lists. Sustained campaigning by David Cameron in opposition had narrowed the gap between Labour and the Conservatives on who could most be trusted to look after the NHS, but this soon widened once the Tories were in office (ending up as a 24-point margin for Labour by the 2015 election campaign). One reason was that many believed the health service was subject to cuts, despite ministers' assurances to the contrary. The other was the Lansley reforms – a reorganisation programme which was widely opposed by health professionals, and which voters found baffling, since they had no idea why such apparently disruptive changes were needed or how they were supposed to benefit patients.

As the economy recovered, however, so did the Conservatives' reputation for economic management. But for struggling voters, the real question was how and when the recovery would reach their own households. With wages stagnant and prices rising, life was hard and showed no signs of getting any easier, despite the upturn they kept hearing about. A similar question arose about the future of austerity. The deficit and the debt sounded big and important, but also somehow intangible, while cuts felt all too real. People who understood that spending restraint was required after 2010 wondered if it was still needed, especially if things were supposed to be looking up. Many also wondered how austerity would ultimately benefit them: what was the end to which cutting the deficit was the means? As I observed on the basis of my research seven months before the election, the Tories' task was to create a "coalition of the willing" – a big enough group of voters prepared to accept continued austerity because they believed the results would be worth waiting for.

Ultimately, this is what they did. According to my post-vote poll conducted on election day in 2015, 84 per cent of those who had voted to put the Tories back into office with an unexpected overall majority agreed that "the economy is not fully fixed so we will need to continue with austerity and cuts in government spending for the next five years". Most others, and the overwhelming majority of Labour voters, thought cuts were no longer necessary or had not been needed in the first place. While just under half of Conservative voters said they were already feeling the effects of the economic recovery, nearly as many again said they were not feeling the benefits yet but expected to at some point.

Taking action on the deficit was by no means the only notable accomplishment of the parliament. Legislation to legalise same-sex marriage, passed in 2013, helped to humanise the party in the eyes of previously suspicious voters – indeed, a YouGov survey at the end of his premiership found that younger people in particular considered this to be David Cameron's single biggest success.

But in the final analysis, three things accounted for the result of the 2015 election. The first was that enough people thought the government was doing a reasonable job, especially on the economy, and ought to be allowed to get on with it. The second was that they liked the way Cameron was performing as Prime Minister. The third was that Labour appeared not to have learned the lessons of its 2010 defeat: many voters worried that putting them back into office would mean going back to square one on the deficit and undoing what had been achieved in areas like welfare reform, and that the Labour leader, Ed Miliband, was just not up to being PM. The Liberal Democrats had lost half their support the moment they went into coalition and never recovered, with many of their former voters feeling the party had not managed to make their presence felt in government. Many who had flirted with UKIP, or even voted for them in mid-term council or European elections, decided to think again when it came to choosing a government.

In other words, the Conservative victory in 2015 came down to competence, leadership and the lack of a plausible alternative. The deeper misgivings that had held the party back for so long had not gone away. If the Tories had come to be seen as the most competent and ready to take hard decisions, they were still well behind Labour when it came to standing for fairness, being on the side of "people like me" and having their heart in the right place. And while the Conservatives were thought better able to run the economy and reduce the deficit, Labour were by far the most trusted on public services like schools and, especially, the NHS. Shortly before the election we asked one of our focus groups of undecided voters to describe what each of the parties would be like if it were a house. The Conservative residence, they said, would have nice thick carpets and "one of those kitchen islands". There would be Hunter wellies in the hall and a "posh dog", probably a chocolate Labrador. But "you can't get to the door because there is an intercom at the gates", and once inside "you have to wipe your feet". Hardly the image the Tories had hoped to cultivate, and probably not much different from the answer we would have heard five years earlier, or even ten.

But why does that matter? The Tories won, didn't they – what difference does it make how they did it? The answer is that a strong brand is like an insurance policy: it means you get the benefit of the doubt when things go wrong. It also means you have a broader basis on which to appeal to people, and that greater numbers will be prepared to give you a hearing. It means you won't be dismissed when the public agenda shifts to a subject on which you might not otherwise be trusted.

So a party can rely for a time on competence, leadership and the absence of opposition. But what if, say, events conspired to call that competence into question? What if the leader were unexpectedly replaced with another who had different qualities? And what if the opposition were to surprise you and get its act together – and you found that to stay in office you had to convince people who had never given you a second look that you were the government for them?

* * *

Fourteen months after the Conservatives' 2015 triumph, the British political landscape looked almost unrecognisably different. A new Prime Minister, a new Cabinet, a new leader of what passed for the opposition, and a Liberal Democrat party with only eight MPs. And the UK had voted to leave the European Union.

On entering Downing Street, Theresa May said she planned to follow David Cameron in leading a "one-nation government", but made clear there were things she wanted to change. She would fight "the burning injustice that, if you're born poor, you will die on average nine years earlier than others. If you're black, you're treated more harshly by the criminal justice system than if you're white. If you're a white, working-class boy, you're less likely than anybody else in Britain to go to university. If you're at a state school, you're less likely to reach the top professions than if you're educated privately. If you're a woman, you will earn less than a man. If you suffer from mental health problems, there's not enough help to hand. If you're young, you'll find it harder than ever before to own your own home." She acknowledged that "if you're from an ordinary working-class family, life is much harder than many people in Westminster realise. You have a job, but you don't always have job security. You have your own home, but you worry about paying a mortgage. You can just about manage, but you worry about the cost of living and getting your kids into a good school." Directly addressing those who were "just managing", she promised that the government she led would "be driven not by the interests of the privileged few, but by yours".

In the weeks that followed, my research found that this had been noticed. Some in our focus groups who were sceptical about the Conservatives said that they would wait to see whether she delivered on it, but that they liked what they had heard: "She attempted to touch base with the regular person. It's too early to say, but I acknowledge that she made an attempt. It's been a while since that happened because they've been in a different world." People's first impressions were that the new PM was capable, tough, realistic, tenacious, smart, direct, confident, sharp and, above all, serious.

Some of these impressions came from Mrs. May's six years as Home Secretary, during which she had, among other things, "got the hook man out of the country" (a reference to the eight-year quest to extradite Abu Hamza to the United States to face terrorism charges). Those with connections to the police recalled her tenure less fondly, but there was also some grudging admiration: "She went to the Police Federation conference and told them what she thought. I totally opposed what she said but that was real strength of character, and that's a sign of what's to come, I think."

The reaction to her style and tone compared to that of her predecessor brought echoes of the handover from Tony Blair to Gordon Brown nine years earlier: "Cameron was a very good PR man, and I don't think she's that bothered with that. She's not going to sugar-coat things." Theresa May's status as the second woman Prime Minister inevitably drew comparisons with Margaret Thatcher ("she's going to be the new Iron Maiden!"). For some, particularly non-Tories, this was a cloud on the horizon – her "aura of strength and power" might turn out to be a good or a bad thing; people hoped she would not "end up steamrollering and being hard-nosed and not listening". All in all, though, "not bad for a Tory".

Most importantly of all for many voters, Theresa May seemed like a leader who was right for the times. Some said they "sighed with relief" when they learned the job was hers. While "Boris would have been funnier" (though it turned out he "didn't have the balls for it"), "we need someone who has been around, who has experience like her, because of everything that's happening at the moment".

Britain's departure from the EU had come to dominate politics. The new PM's mantra that "Brexit means Brexit" successfully signalled her determination to honour the referendum result despite having campaigned for a remain vote. At the same time, it left people none the wiser as to what Brexit would mean in practice, or what kind of deal she would be aiming to achieve. Research I conducted as the government prepared to trigger Article 50, the formal two-year process of leaving the EU – and published ten days before the surprise announcement of an early general election – found people confused or at odds over the kind of agreement that should be pursued.

If the negotiations came down to a balance between access to the European single market and the ability to control immigration from EU countries, most people, including two thirds of those who voted to leave, would choose the latter. Indeed, remainers often agreed that continuing with unfettered free movement would effectively mean ignoring the democratically expressed wishes of the country. But many, especially leave voters, argued that no such trade-off really existed at all. Since Europe benefited from free trade by selling more to us than we do to them, they asked, why would we need to make concessions for it to continue? Asked about four potential negotiating aims – ending contributions to the EU budget, no longer being subject to rulings from the European Court of Justice, being able to pick and choose which EU nationals were allowed to live and work in Britain, and continued tariff-free trade with EU countries – leave voters thought each one was not only very important but more likely than not to be achieved. Whatever the technicalities, leavers were fairly confident that Theresa May would get a good deal for Britain (though remainers slightly less so, not least because many thought the UK would have the weaker hand in negotiations whoever was in charge).

Either way, most said they would rather see Theresa May and the Conservatives batting for Britain than their opponents. The Labour Party, according to previous Labour voters who took part in our research in the early months of the May government, was "a catastrophe", "a basket case" and "a farce". It was no longer made up of ordinary working people but "students, extremists, the far left". Jeremy Corbyn, chosen by Labour's members and registered supporters to replace Ed Miliband as leader in September 2015, having started as a hundred-to-one outsider, was "totally unelectable", "unprofessional", "too far to the left", "the greatest thing for the Tory party that ever happened". Though a decent enough individual, he was an activist rather than a leader. As one frustrated supporter put it, Labour had to be "more than just a social movement – you've got to be able to get in and make the changes". No one saw any prospect of that happening.

By huge margins, the Conservatives were regarded as being more competent, willing to take tough decisions for the long term, and clear about what they stood for. They were way ahead on nearly all policy issues, especially cutting the deficit, negotiating Brexit, crime, welfare reform and managing the economy. Despite their disarray, however, Labour were still thought to be much more committed to fairness, opportunity for all, and helping ordinary people get on in life. And, just as in 2015, they were also more trusted to improve the NHS, the most important issue for voters when asked what mattered to them and their family, rather than to the country as a whole.

In the twelve years since the ignominy of their third defeat, the Conservative Party's fortunes were transformed. The Tories looked electorally unassailable; the more pertinent question, asked on the left as much as anywhere, was whether the Labour Party would survive. The Conservative Party had not only clawed its way back to a majority in the House of Commons, but to complete command of the political landscape. Such was the scene as Mr. and Mrs. May departed for a short walking holiday in the Welsh hills just before Easter in 2017. What could possibly go wrong?

2 / The campaign (as seen by the voters)

"YOU'RE JOKING?! NOT ANOTHER ONE? Oh for God's sake, I honestly, I can't stand this." Brenda from Bristol, as she became known to the nation, spoke for millions when told by a local television reporter of Theresa May's shock announcement. "There's too much politics going on at the moment," she continued. "Why does she need to do it?"

The Prime Minister's answer, which she gave in a surprise Downing Street press conference on Tuesday 18th April, was that there was division in Westminster at a time when there should be unity. In recent weeks, she said, Labour had threatened to vote against the final Brexit deal the government reached with the EU, the Liberal Democrats had said they wanted to grind the business of government to a standstill, the Scottish National Party had pledged to vote against legislation formally repealing Britain's EU membership, and "unelected members of the House of Lords have vowed to fight us every step of the way". Such "game playing" weakened the country's negotiating position in Europe, "so we need a general election and we need one now, because we have at this moment a one-off chance to get this done while the European Union agrees its negotiating position and before the detailed talks begin". She acknowledged that she had had a change of heart on the question: "Since I became Prime Minister I have said that there should be no election until 2020, but now I have concluded that the only way to guarantee certainty and stability for the years ahead is to hold this election and seek your support for the decisions I must take."

Many voters greeted this explanation with some scepticism, to say the very least, judging from the first of the focus groups we conducted around the country three nights a week throughout the campaign. One typical response: "I think it's a bit cheeky… She was obviously trying to seize the situation. To go when Labour's at the lowest they've been does seem a bit opportunistic."

This interpretation of the PM's real reasons for going to the country early had two important implications for the voters who held it. The first was that she thought it obvious that she would win with a bigger majority than she had now, which made her seem complacent, or "a bit too cocky". The second was that it suggested she was willing to break her word if she thought it was in her narrow political interest to do so: "It makes me feel I can't trust her, because she said again and again, 'I will not do this', and then she changes her mind."

For some others, there was a feeling that it was simply too soon to be going back to the polls: "It's all happening too fast. Normally you have three or four years to digest what the government is doing… We've had one huge major decision in Brexit very recently, and all of a sudden we're making another." Or, to put it another way, "I don't know what I'm buying, do I? I haven't seen you perform yet." This particular reaction was also an early warning that many would want to think about more than Brexit when deciding how to vote.

All about Brexit?

Not everyone was cynical about Theresa May's professed motives. Those already more sympathetic to the PM were inclined to give her the benefit of the doubt, especially if they also agreed that Brexit was the pre-eminent issue of the moment: "I believe she's not getting the support she needs to leave… There is so much discord happening in the political world, so many other parties and leaders going against Theresa May, so she wants to show the other side 'the people are with me, I'm going to do what I have to do'."

For large numbers of voters, the looming Brexit negotiations put the issue inescapably at the top of the agenda, whether or not they approved of the early election, whether or not they had voted Conservative before, and however they voted in the referendum. Some saw it as the most important issue they could remember being at stake in an election: "Working from the age of sixteen up until now I'm fifty, no matter who's been in parliament it hasn't changed what I earn, it hasn't changed where I live." But this time, "it matters because of Brexit, because it's a huge thing for this country. So I'm thinking of the best person to take us through that."

"At the moment I believe in more of Labour's policies, but if it's about Brexit, Theresa May."

For most people who saw things in this light, the person in question was Theresa May: "For as long as I can remember I'd never think about voting Conservative, but I think the most important issue is Brexit, I think Labour scrapping and restarting it would not be beneficial to the UK, I don't agree with the Lib Dems trying to do the vote again, because the people have spoken and that's how it should be even if I disagree with it, and the Conservatives I think are in the best position to negotiate us a deal;" "At the moment I believe in more of Labour's policies, but if it's about Brexit, Theresa May."

Apart from anything else, the alternative seemed unthinkable, even to many previous Labour voters: "I can't imagine Jeremy Corbyn sitting with twenty-seven EU leaders on the other side;" "Corbyn is too much of a gentleman. I don't think he'd push it too far, he'd accept the middle ground, and possibly not to our best advantage;" "Labour would kind of pander to what other people want and kind of mess it up in the end;" "Jeremy doesn't want to upset anybody, he wants to go out holding hands with everybody, and I don't think that's going to be the best deal for our country. I think she'll dig her heels in a bit more."

This line of argument did not work for everyone, and for two main reasons. The first, often expounded by remain voters unreconciled to Brexit, was that it hardly mattered who did the negotiating: Britain would get what it was given. "She's trying to say 'this is the deal we want', but it will be, 'no, these are our terms – we'll tell you how it's going to go now'." After all, "they don't want the EU to break up, so they can't give us a good deal;" "We're outnumbered, we're in a parlous position. We'll rue the day, whoever is leading the so-called negotiations."

The second was that Brexit was not at the top of everyone's agenda. Participants in our groups mentioned a wide variety of other things they wanted addressed – including school funding, housing, tax, the environment, local issues, public sector pay and seemingly perpetual austerity – none of which seemed to be high on the Conservatives' agenda.

Some said they were in a dilemma over whether to choose the best person to lead on Brexit and, in doing so, vote for less desirable things that might come as part of the Tory package. "We're going to get absolutely hammered by the other twenty-seven countries, and we need someone strong to give us the best deal. But I also think she will, at the same time, put a lot more right-wing policies in place in the UK;" "I just feel worried. I don't know if I would a hundred per cent want to vote for the Conservatives, because still emotionally I'm attached to Labour. But at the same time, because I'm fearful about what is going to happen once we Brexit, I almost feel if I don't vote for them and someone else gets in and it gets interrupted, we might end up in a worse position. Because of that fear, I'm sort of stuck."

The party of the 7.4 per cent

The Conservatives were not alone in putting Brexit at the forefront of their campaign. The Liberal Democrats, traditionally the most enthusiastic about the European Union, saw the issue as their route to recovery. Having gone into the previous election with 57 seats and come out with eight, they set their sights on the remain-voting half of the country, campaigning to keep Britain in the single market and promising a second referendum on the final Brexit deal, thereby allowing voters the chance to "change direction" and stay in the EU. This approach won the party just four extra seats (or a fifty per cent increase, depending on how you look at it), albeit an even lower share of the vote than the eight per cent they secured in 2015.

Three main reasons emerged from our campaign focus groups as to why the Lib Dems did not achieve their aim of becoming "the party of the 48 per cent". The first of these is that those who voted to remain did not necessarily support the idea of trying to reverse the decision. Time and again in our groups, remain voters said the will of the people had to be respected: "It's like in Ireland, where they said no, and then they went, 'oh no, that's the wrong one, you must vote again'. I don't think it would help, particularly, I think people have decided."

"I think he's principled, I just don't agree with his principles."

Second, since their 2015 wipeout the Lib Dems had disappeared from many voters' radars. Our participants often said they had heard little or nothing from the party since the last election. Apart from their position on Brexit, the only Lib Dem policies our participants could recall were legalising cannabis and scrapping diesel cars; apart from this,

"I don't know what else they'd get up to." Very few had an opinion about the party leader, Tim Farron ("to be honest, I don't even know his name"; "I think he's principled, I just don't agree with his principles"); the party just seemed too small and irrelevant to make any difference on a national scale. For those in our groups who were leaning towards the party, their opinion on Brexit usually coincided with an already favourable view of their local candidate. As a lady in Twickenham said, "if I vote for Vince, there's no way the Lib Dems are going to run the whole country. But I quite like Vince and I like what he does locally." Expecting a potential Tory landslide, some were also thinking of voting for the party "to provide some sort of balance… I think it will be Theresa May on 8th June, but you can think why people would vote Lib Dem to counterbalance that."

Third, the militant remainers the Lib Dems were aiming to target were more likely than most to be anti-Tory. Many of them therefore had bitter memories of what they regarded as the betrayals and broken promises of the Cameron–Clegg coalition: "I don't think people have forgotten what the Lib Dems did by joining the Conservatives. I haven't."

The unlikely insurgency

In an interview with LBC on 2 May, the Shadow Home Secretary, Diane Abbott, got in a muddle over the details of Labour's plan to recruit 10,000 new police officers. Pressed by Nick Ferrari on the cost of the proposal, she initially gave a figure of £300,000, implying they would each be paid £30 a year, before going on to suggest the number of new officers would be 250,000. The political stories that make the biggest impression on the public are nearly always those which the politicians who feature in them wish had never happened, and this was a prime example. The incident was mentioned spontaneously in nearly every one of our focus groups from then until election day. Though people often said they sympathised with Ms. Abbott over the blunder and its endless repetition on the media, it crystallised many people's view of Labour's basic competence and apparently cavalier attitude to public money: "It just shows what she's like. What Labour's like;" "Diane Abbott! I know she got trapped in a difficult situation, but the level of politician they have in the Labour Party is not the quality they had in the past;" "They have no clue about anything;" "The party's in disarray. I mean, do they even have a stance on Brexit? I don't know."

> ***"He's anti-military. He wants nuclear submarines without the nuclear missiles. How stupid can that be?"***

For many undecided voters, this problem extended all the way up to the leadership. Indeed, lifelong Labour voters would often say that Jeremy Corbyn was the single biggest reason they were reluctant to stay with the party. Some had political objections: "He's anti-military. He wants nuclear submarines without the nuclear missiles. How stupid can that be?"; "It's disastrous, his stance on defence, potentially catastrophic;" "He had links with the IRA. I didn't like that at all;" "He said was doing peace talks, but he wasn't doing peace talks. He was supporting the IRA. He was turning up at IRA gunmen's funerals."

More often, though, people simply did not think he was up to the job of leading the country: "It's not necessarily that I don't like him; I don't have confidence in him. I don't think he's a strong enough person. I don't agree with everything he says, but then I don't agree with everything any of them say. I just think he's wet." Some felt this weakness as a leader was a result of his virtues: "He's too principled. You need to be pragmatic and sneaky like the Tories to get anywhere;" "I think he's the most humanitarian of all our politicians… But that could be our problem with Corbyn. He's just going to give it all away;" "The sentiment's behind it, he knows what he wants to do, but I'm not convinced he's the one that will be able to make it happen… You can't imagine him being up there with all the other world leaders;" "He's a gentleman, isn't he? That's his problem, that he's a gentleman." Values were all very well, but "you need a leader, otherwise it's wishy-washy;" "I couldn't see him as Prime Minister, could you? Could anybody? Theresa May has got more balls. He just hasn't got it in him." People also noted that their doubts seemed to be shared by many of Corbyn's own MPs: "If they didn't have the confidence in him, then how are we meant to have confidence?"

"I think he is actually handling the whole negative portrayal of himself in the media, standing up quite well to that. He's won me over a little bit by his presence."

It was notable, however, that the things our participants said about Jeremy Corbyn became more positive as the campaign progressed. Several people said that once they started to listen to him, they began to feel that the prevailing media characterisation of him was unfair: "I've gone from not really wanting to vote to being more pro-Labour, just because I think he is actually handling the whole negative portrayal of himself in the media, standing up quite well to that. He's won me over a little bit by his presence;" "I saw him on the *Andrew Marr Show*, and I was sitting there thinking, 'actually, you're making a lot of sense, and I kind of agree with quite a lot of what you're saying'. And that slightly surprised me;" "When I started to listen to him being interviewed and him actually talking, I had a slightly different impression of him. I think up until then I had bought into, oh, he's weak and not really going to be effective in any way." People sometimes added that they had been impressed with the dignified way in which he had dealt with such hostility: "I think he's also shown that he's got very thick skin and he's quite resilient, and he's quite a fighter. And he seemed to stay true to his values throughout his political career."

"If you asked me a year ago if Jeremy Corbyn would make a good Prime Minister, I'd have laughed, because he was just a shambolic joke. But he's transformed himself."

As the weeks went by, a theme developed in our focus groups that the more people saw of Corbyn on the campaign trail and the better they got to know him, the more they liked him: "I read somewhere that he claimed about £1.75 for a bus fare last year and didn't claim anything else… If you look at the front of his house you can see he's not into possessions and stuff;" "He's started to dress properly, recently, started to put a shirt and tie on;" "If you asked me a year ago if Jeremy Corbyn would make a good Prime Minister, I'd have laughed, because he was just a shambolic joke. But he's transformed himself. He's been so impressive in the debates;" "He's like that person at school you really, really hate, but when you get to know them you find they're actually quite cool."

Labour's manifesto, leaked on 11th May and formally launched five days later, clearly enthused many of the party's otherwise reluctant potential voters. Many participants had heard about particular issues or policies that appealed to them personally: "Housing – I think that's the thing that's stood out for me because I rent. Labour are promising to protect private renters and make more affordable properties for first-time buyers;" "He's saying to me the things that have wound me up for ages, like large corporations like Amazon getting away with not paying their taxes and going offshore and all the rest of it;" "To me, I think he's returning to traditional Labour values. So I understand him wanting to do things like renationalising the railways, put more money into education, get rid of tuition fees;" "A lot of the welfare rights stuff – potentially increasing the carers' allowance to be in line with Job Seekers' Allowance, and policies towards sanctions on benefits, because I see a lot of that in my work;" "Nationalising the Royal Mail, that would be brilliant. We'd be getting seven hundred million quid profit a year, and none of it going into the coffers of shareholders."

"I've had two one per cent pay rises in seven years, and he's going to scrap the freeze on public pay. So even though I think she's the best for the job and the best party to lead the Brexit, I'll most probably vote for Labour again."

One of the biggest attractions, which our participants raised spontaneously throughout the campaign, was Labour's pledge to scrap the cap on public sector pay. Some were candid enough to say this was a powerful enough inducement to override all other considerations: "I was thinking of voting for her until this morning, because I think she's more sensible. But I work for Birmingham City Council, and I've had two one per cent pay rises in seven years, I think. And he's going to scrap the freeze on public pay. So when I get to the voting station, even though I think she's the best for the job and the best party to lead the Brexit, I'll most probably vote for Labour again."

At the same time, the Labour manifesto found plenty of sceptics. There were three main kinds of doubt. First, following on from their reservations about Labour's leadership and competence, was the question of whether the party would be able to enact such an ambitious agenda: "It's what I want to hear. As a working-class person it's directed at me – the schools, the hospitals, old age… He's saying the right things, but I don't think he's got the party behind him to see things through;" "If he did win, he'd sit down at his table with his pen and go, 'oh God, now I've got to do all this'."

Second, some were worried that the programme represented a break with Labour's generally moderate recent history, or that it would put off centrist voters: "We've had a lot of Labour governments that I thought were progressive, moving towards the middle, trying to be what I considered reasonably fair. But he seems to have gone much further to the left. I've never wanted to be carried or carry anyone, I've just wanted to have a reasonably level playing field where I can ply my skills, time, trade, effort, and it seems that he's saying, 'no, no, everyone should have everything';" "They went too far to the left, Corbyn and the people around him, John McDonnell and Diane Abbott. They're just not going to win the centre ground, and that's what they need to win. I mean, I'm a socialist, but you've got to be practical."

The third and most common doubt was over how Labour's plans would be paid for: "The NHS haven't got enough money anyway, so how is he going to sort out free parking?"; "They're saying a £10 an hour minimum wage… I don't know how they're going to achieve that without people losing their jobs." As for free university tuition, "is that realistic? Can the country afford to subsidise so heavily?" (and in any case, as one Labour-leaning participant put it, "people need to pay their way in life"). People wanted to hear "that there's going to be more policemen and we want to hear that the NHS is going to get God knows how much money. We want to hear all those things, but none of it stacks up." People also debated the merits of raising taxes on incomes over £80,000: many thought it was fair, but such an income was hardly a fortune given the housing market in the south, and in any case "you get them tax evaders, like that comedian with the beady eyes". At the same time, people were suspicious of Labour's promise that no one earning less than this would have to pay more: "I'd probably respect him more if he said 'look, we want to do all these things but it's going to cost everyone something in their income tax,' rather than say 'oh, we're just going to tax the rich,' because it's never going to happen." For some, the party's message amounted to no more than "vote Labour and we'll give you a free kitten. Because when you look at everything they've promised and everything they've said, I think they're just telling us what we want to hear."

Labour's spending promises reminded many undecided voters of the condition of the public finances at the end of Gordon Brown's government: "He can promise us everything, but the mess they got us into before by promising so much and giving so much has got to where we are now where the purse strings have had to be tightened so much." But some, echoing our Birmingham City Council worker, were only interested in how the policies would affect them personally, not their impact on the Treasury: "We're too far down the ladder to know the difference."

Strong and stable?

"Strong and stable leadership" was a humdrum slogan than nevertheless summed up what many neutrals felt about Theresa May at the outset of the campaign. In the nine months since she became Prime Minister people had come to see her as a serious and capable leader, who brought a bracing change in style from that of her predecessor: "She's not as much of a spin-merchant as David Cameron was. She seems quite forthright and clear-thinking. She's just a straightforward politician. And you might not agree with her views on everything, but I think she says everything in firm belief."

At the beginning of the campaign there was also a widespread feeling that she was a different kind of Conservative. Some traced this back to her first speech in Downing Street on taking office, in which she spoke about tackling injustice and the need to help those who "can just about manage" but who worry about job security, the cost of living and public services. These priorities had made an impression on many of the undecided voters in our groups: "It sounds like she's not just for people who have got higher incomes, she's for everyone;" "She comes across as being for the working class, which I think is quite unusual." Whereas the Tories had once "seemed like royalty stepping out of their palaces" with "no clue how we lived", the PM had "worked her way up from the ground to where she is now, so she does represent somebody who is hard-working. She isn't one who has been, what do they say, born with a silver spoon."

"Theresa May voted remain, but she's accepted the vote like a lot of people haven't, and she's saying 'I'm going to do it because that's what the majority voted for'."

The idea that the Conservatives might be taking more of an interest in ordinary people was further boosted by the fact that the government, and the PM in particular, seemed determined to implement the will of the public as expressed in the EU referendum – something they were not used to seeing in politics: "Nobody believes politicians full-stop, really. But at the end of the day, we've seen something we voted for happen… They can say 'we'll look after the NHS,' but they never do, you know they're not going to. But with this, it's happened." This was all the more commendable given that the PM herself had campaigned for a different outcome: "You look at Theresa May, and she voted remain, but she's accepted the vote like a lot of people haven't, and she's saying 'I'm going to do it because that's what the majority voted for'." This also underlined her credentials as a strong leader: "I think she's stood firm in what the people have asked for. I think if Labour were in charge we would have backtracked a little bit;" "She's very hard-nosed. She's tough. She's got a bit of backbone."

"She called the snap election, and now she can't be bothered turning up to it."

As the campaign went on, however, these very positive views became much more mixed. People noticed that her appearances looked very tightly controlled, and some thought she seemed ill-at-ease meeting ordinary members of the public – a contrast with Jeremy Corbyn, who seemed to become more natural and relaxed by the day: "I don't find her relatable at all… When she starts talking it's like she's reading a script;" "She tries to come across in that Thatcher directorial tone, but can't actually deliver it. It comes across like a false front;" "Labour events are all public, anybody can turn up. What the Conservative Party are doing is handpicking. There's an area of Leeds called Harehills, which is probably one of the most multicultural areas you'll find in the country, and the Conservative leader's organised her event there and it was a pure white hand-picked audience in the middle of Harehills. At Labour events, people can just turn up. She would not stand in the middle of the street and do her campaign." These impressions combined to cast the PM's decision not to take part in head-to-head television debates in the worst possible light: "If she'd done the debates she'd have been ripped to shreds;" "She called the snap election, and now she can't be bothered turning up to it."

If Labour's policy platform galvanised the party's wavering voters, the Conservative manifesto, launched two days later, made a number of potential Tories think twice. There were isolated mentions in our focus groups of welcome policies on mental health, parental leave, and the proposed energy price cap, but recall of Tory plans among our participants was dominated by five areas: scrapping the "triple lock" whereby pensions rise at the same rate as earnings, prices, or at 2.5 per cent, whichever is highest; means-testing the Winter Fuel Payment; ending free school lunches for all infants and replacing them with free breakfasts; reforming social care funding so that £100,000 of a pensioner's assets would be protected (but including their home in the calculation of those assets in the case of domiciliary care, as was already the case with residential care); and a free vote in parliament on fox hunting.

Some of these policies had their defenders – why should children get free lunches if their parents can afford to pay, why should Winter Fuel Payments go to pensioners who don't need them, and isn't protecting assets of £100,000 better than the current arrangement? – but all in all, it sounded to many in our groups like a pretty grim package: "Three or four weeks ago when the general election first came about, I was going to vote Conservative for the first time ever. But since the manifesto she brought out about getting rid of free school meals for children… Some people in this country, that's the child's only hot meal of the day;" "They promised a triple lock on pensions and that's getting scrapped, and my dad's getting on and saying he might have to sell his house to fund his care." The characterisation of the proposed social care reform as a "Dementia Tax" was devastatingly effective: "The Dementia Tax, that seems pretty bad. I don't think it's very nice, preying on those that need it… Those that are suffering dementia and have got some money are getting taxed on their healthcare for dementia. Have I got that right?"

Four days after the manifesto launch, Mrs. May announced what was widely regarded as a U-turn on the policy. While claiming that "nothing has changed", she stressed at a campaign event in Wales that the new plan would include an absolute cap on the sum people would have to pay for care, as well as a floor on the amount of savings they would be left with. This did little to improve the situation: "She said there was a cap, and then no, there wasn't a cap, and then there was a cap. It just makes them seem unreliable and less, I don't know, honest somehow." It also reminded people of previous reversals, making the government seem anything but strong and stable: "That's quite a few U-turns she's done. She said she'd never announce a general election, and all of a sudden she announced a general election. She U-turned on quite a few things before that as well, like National Insurance;" "It's like in the Budget, things are pushed through and then suddenly it's like, 'oh, you didn't like it, we'll take it back'."

"There's nothing positive. They're just saying that they can manage the Brexit better."

Though people were used to governments having to make tough decisions, our groups often remarked that the Conservatives seemed to have nothing to offer, or at least nothing they had heard about, that would make a tangible difference to their lives. While Labour were trying to show "that they're for everybody, rather than the chosen few", or "saving everyone a ton of money", the only argument the Tories seemed to be making for a blue vote was "Brexit Brexit Brexit Brexit": "There's nothing positive. They're just saying that they can manage the Brexit better." As we have already seen, many people found this was not enough: "To be honest with you, I don't care about the outside world and what goes on – all I care about is the four walls of my house and how it's going to affect me and my kids."

The impression that the party was planning to take away more than they were offering helped to reawaken underlying concerns about the Tories' character and motives among people who had thought about backing Theresa May: "They feel quite far removed, I feel, from the average working person, just historically, background and things like that;" "I would struggle to accept the Tories telling me that their policies would make for a fairer Britain;" "A third of the *Sunday Times* Rich List actually donated to the Conservative Party;" "She spent a thousand pounds on a pair of trousers, didn't she?"

"She's on about bringing back fox hunting. I mean, what's that? Tally-ho and running up and down and ripping foxes to pieces for the élite."

Judging from our participants, nothing did more to reinforce old impressions of the Tory brand than the prospect of reintroducing fox hunting. In group after group, people would say they had seen something about the issue on Facebook, suggesting an orchestrated campaign, and an effective one at that: "She's on about bringing back fox hunting. I mean, what's that? Tally-ho and running up and down and ripping foxes to pieces for the élite;" "I'm undecided because I just heard that May is on about bringing back fox hunting, and I'm against that." Still, some people declared themselves resistant to friends using social media to persuade them: "It's literally winding me up, actually… I'm thinking, do you know what, I don't know if I even want to vote for Labour, because you're telling me to vote. I'll vote for who I want to vote for."

Angel of the North

In Scotland, meanwhile, the Scottish National Party's strident opposition to Brexit and desire to keep Scotland in the EU had led some of its previous voters to look elsewhere: "I can't vote SNP, because of the simple reason that I voted to leave Europe. So why leave the UK to be run by Europe?" Indeed, for those who had voted SNP in 2015 but were now looking for an alternative, the party's apparently dogged pursuit of the independence agenda – Nicola Sturgeon having argued that a vote for EU withdrawal against Scotland's wishes could be grounds for a second independence referendum – was the single biggest reason.

"Independence was meant to be a once-in-a-generation vote, they'd respect the opinion of the people, people voted no, and they're pushing for another one. So I think a lot of people lost faith."

This suggested several things about the Scottish Nationalists and their leader. The first was that they did not, after all, seem all that devoted to the people's will: "It was meant to be a once-in-a-generation vote, they'd respect the opinion of the people, people voted no, and they're pushing for another one. So I think a lot of people lost faith;" "She had her vote and it didn't happen for her, but she still hasn't let it go. She still keeps banging on about it at any opportunity she gets." Another was that what they saw as the SNP's single-mindedness made the party seem out of touch with the times: "We've got bigger problems at the minute, like Brexit… Just now, when there's bigger stuff going on nationwide, I think we have to look at the bigger picture, and for me personally that's why I've gone away from the SNP just now." Yet another was the feeling that the independence agenda had led the party to neglect priorities at Holyrood that many voters felt were closer to home: "Every time Nicola Sturgeon is on the television she's banging on about the referendum to go solo, but she wants to be concentrating on things like the NHS, that's in absolute chaos, education, absolutely awful. One of my grandchildren has not had a decent teacher this whole year;" "It's the fact that the SNP haven't really delivered. They said a lot of things they would do, and they haven't. They can talk the talk but they can't walk the walk."

And in Aberdeen in particular, the collapse in the oil price had led some to question the assumptions behind the independence argument. Though they did not blame the SNP government for the industry's plight, they did think it made the idea of an independent Scotland seem somewhat more risky: "The SNP was all about the oil. Should they not have been more informed than we were about things like that? Should they not have known that the oil was about to go on a downturn?"

There were also doubts as to the effectiveness of the SNP's huge delegation at Westminster: "What impact they can have in terms of votes in the House of Commons I'm not sure, but it's a voice;" "They cost a fortune. If you look at the table between the expenses of their predecessors and how much they've claimed on their expenses, it's outrageous, absolutely outrageous – three, four times as much. They've got their nose in the trough."

Such criticism of Scotland's biggest party was far from universal. Many still liked and admired Nicola Sturgeon, and people noted that the SNP still seemed the most visible and active party on the ground. However, as with Labour in England, many said they found its online supporters wearying: "I've got a few Facebook friends who are just mad SNP pro-indy… I just put them on 'ignore'. I actually hovered over 'unfollow';" "It's like getting a cheese grater dragged down your face."

"She's more of a Scottish Conservative, as opposed to an English Conservative in Scotland."

Many of those who were looking for an alternative to the SNP were hesitant about going to Labour, either because of its leadership or what they saw as the implausibility of its manifesto commitments. For many, this left one viable option: "I hate to say it, but the Tories." A combination of Labour's demoralised state in Scotland and the performance of Ruth Davidson had left the Conservatives as the "natural opposition" to the SNP. The Scottish Tory leader was praised on all sides (even if "she talks too fast"): "I find her quite listenable. She's very engaging;" "I've never voted Tory but she's got what I think is missing UK-wide, that likeability factor;" "It's her personality. She's done comedy shows, and she comes across as a great leader;" "Her Twitter game is strong." Importantly, for a party often associated with England, "she's more of a Scottish Conservative, as opposed to an English Conservative in Scotland."

This likeability did not detract from her seriousness. "I think she can say what she needs to say. I think if she's got something to put across, she will say it;" "Somebody's got to stand up to Nicola, and she can stand toe to toe with her."

The biscuit of truth

To conclude each of our focus groups, we asked participants to think about the party leaders in a different way, in an attempt to understand what was at the back of their minds when they pondered their prospective Prime Ministers. If Jeremy Corbyn were an animal, for example, what kind of animal would he be? "An anteater. He kind of resembles one, for some reason. But it's more the manner of an anteater. It's not kind of get-up-and-go, it's kind of in its place, isn't it, the anteater?" "A cat. Not a wild-cat." "Maybe a meerkat. He stands up on his legs and looks around when something's happening, but then goes back down again." "A sheepdog, an old English sheepdog. I think because he rides a bike and he's a vegetarian and things like that, I find him quite approachable and kind of shaggy." And Theresa May? "An owl. Sits in her tree and gets on with it. Astute." "What are those dogs that look like wolves? Huskies." "You know,

I think huskies are quite gentle, and I don't think she's gentle. I think she's more of an Alsatian. She barks, but to really bite to the bone, I don't think she's there yet." "I was thinking a bull. Strong, standing her ground." "I'd say a bull. She kind of runs with her ideas and nobody dares to stand in her way, so you just have to accept it's Theresa May and just let her do what she wants, really."

"He's like an old English sheepdog. I think because he rides a bike and he's a vegetarian and things like that, I find him quite approachable and kind of shaggy."

What if the Leader of the Opposition were a cartoon character? "Deputy Dog." "Daffy Duck." "Andy Capp." "I know he's not a cartoon character, but who's the scarecrow guy? Worzel Gummidge." "Shaggy from *Scooby-Doo.*" "Yes, I do get that Jesus-sandal vibe from Jeremy Corbyn, definitely." How about Theresa May? "Lady Penelope." "Her from *101 Dalmatians.* Cruella de Vil." "The head teacher in *Matilda.* Miss Trunchbull. She was really evil, wasn't she? I think Theresa May might have an evil streak in her. If she loses her temper, trust me, them men are going to know about it."

"Theresa May would be the head teacher in Matilda. Miss Trunchbull...
If she loses her temper, trust me, them men are going to know about it."

Who would play the Labour leader in a film of his life? "Harvey Keitel." "John Thaw, when he weren't dead." "Mr. Bean." "Geoffrey Palmer." "Alec Guinness as Obi-Wan Kenobi." "*Steptoe & Son*, the old fella. Wilfrid Brambell." "Compo, from *Last of the Summer Wine.*" And who would take the title role in *Theresa May: The Movie*? "Who plays M in the Bond movies? Judi Dench." "Joanna Lumley. She could get the part across." "Penelope Keith." "Helen Mirren." "I think she's more of a Meryl Streep." "Meryl Streep in *The Devil Wears Prada.*"

How about if they were not in politics at all? What job would Jeremy Corbyn have were he not an MP? "A union leader." "Some non-existent job." "Something in human rights." "Someone who works in a school, teaching sociology, or theology." And what would Mrs. May be? "Corbyn's boss, as headmistress. In a girls' private school. It would be very disciplined. She'd be like Miss Hardbroom in *The Worst Witch.*"

On a more metaphysical level, what about if they were not people, but drinks. Corbyn? "A smoothie or something, made out of something organic and foul." "Ale. A down-to-earth pint. Something your dad would drink, your Grampy." "Bitter lemon. Because he's bitter, and a lemon." And May? "Baileys or prosecco, because she's sophisticated, she's classy." "Strong builder's tea that you forgot to drink and now it's gone cold." "A glass of water. You need it to survive, but there's nothing to it." "A double vodka. Comes with a kick."

And if Jeremy Corbyn were a biscuit? "A Jammie Dodger. He dodges all the important questions." "A custard cream. It's not something you'd go, 'ooh, I want a custard cream'. I'd take it if it was given to me, I wouldn't choose it off the shelf." "Bourbon. The kind that nobody really wants but it's often the only one left." "Hard tack army rations. They taste horrible, they don't fill you up, they're not much use for anything." "A digestive. A nice and comforting digestive." And the Prime Minister? "A Marks & Spencer selection." "A Jaffa Cake. She's nice on the outside, but I don't like the middle of a Jaffa Cake." "A cookie. They're tough, but they crumble." "One of them hard ones at the bottom of the tin that have been there six months. It looks quite nice but you bite it and break all your teeth."

3 / **What happened and why**

FOR AT LEAST the fourth general election in a row, the forecast from the exit poll drew gasps of incredulity throughout Westminster and across the country. Far from the commanding majority on which the Conservatives had gambled, they would be the largest party in a hung parliament. Tory sources continued to dispute the projections until, as the night wore on, evidence from real results became overwhelming. In the event, once again, the exit poll had done its job with remarkable accuracy: the Conservatives ended the night with 318 seats, eight short of an overall majority and thirteen fewer than they had won two years earlier, despite 12 gains in Scotland. Labour were up by 30, to 262; the SNP were down from 56 to 35; the Lib Dems went from eight to 12; UKIP, the SDLP and the Ulster Unionists lost all their MPs, while Sinn Fein and the Democratic Unionists, crucially, rose to seven and ten respectively.

At 42.4 per cent, the Conservative vote share matched that of Margaret Thatcher in her 144-seat victory in 1983. The Tory vote total, 13,669,883, beat the number cast for New Labour in Tony Blair's 1997 landslide. In any other recent election, such a level of support would have given the party that achieved it a sizeable majority (in 2005, Labour won by 66 seats with just 35 per cent of the vote). What none of the parties and few of the pollsters expected was that Labour would be less than 800,000 votes behind, with 40 per cent of the national share.

On election day, I surveyed over 14,000 people after they had voted, to help understand how this extraordinary result had come about. The purpose of the exercise had been to find out what led people to decide as they did and to compare the profile of each party's supporters, rather than to try and project the outcome before the votes were counted, but as it turned out this unweighted post-vote poll came very close to the actual national vote shares: 41 per cent in our survey had voted Conservative, and 39 per cent Labour. This lends credibility to the poll's other findings. While men taking part in my survey had voted Conservative by 43 per cent to 35 per cent, women had backed Labour over the Tories by a two-point margin. Two thirds of 18 to 24 year-olds had voted Labour, but so had more than half of those aged 25 to 34. Only in age groups above 55 did voters break decisively for the Conservative Party.

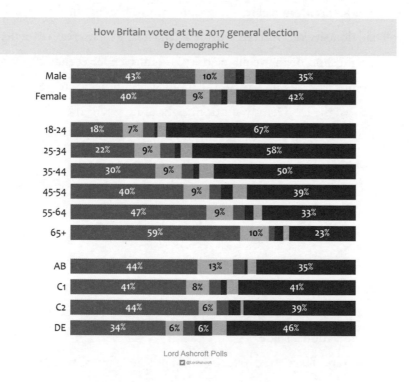

How Britain voted at the 2017 general election
By demographic

Male	43% 10%	35%
Female	40% 9%	42%
18-24	18% 7%	67%
25-34	22% 9%	58%
35-44	30% 9%	50%
45-54	40% 9%	39%
55-64	47% 9%	33%
65+	59% 10%	23%
AB	44% 13%	35%
C1	41% 8%	41%
C2	44% 6%	39%
DE	34% 6% 6%	46%

Lord Ashcroft Polls
@LordAshcroft

The Conservative campaign received few plaudits, and as I described in the previous chapter, we found in our focus groups that undecided voters became more sympathetic to Labour and less sure about the Tories as the weeks went by. This is also borne out by the finding in our post-vote survey that more than half of those who voted Labour made their decision in the month before polling day, and more than a quarter in "the last few days". Conservatives were more likely to have known how they would vote before the campaign started.

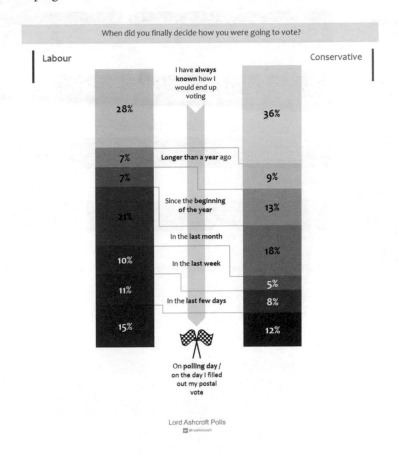

When did you finally decide how you were going to vote?

Labour — Conservative

	Labour	Conservative
I have **always known** how I would end up voting	28%	36%
Longer than a year ago	7%	
	7%	9%
Since the **beginning of the year**	21%	13%
In the **last month**		18%
In the **last week**	10%	5%
In the **last few days**	11%	8%
On **polling day** / on the day I filled out my postal vote	15%	12%

Lord Ashcroft Polls
@LordAshcroft

By the same token, voters who made their minds up towards the end of the campaign were more likely to have gone for Jeremy Corbyn's party than for the Tories.

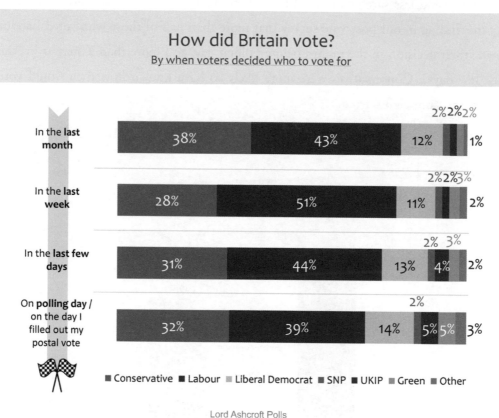

How did Britain vote?
By when voters decided who to vote for

When decided	Conservative	Labour	Liberal Democrat	SNP	UKIP	Green	Other
In the **last month**	38%	43%	12%	2%	2%	2%	1%
In the **last week**	28%	51%	11%	2%	2%	3%	2%
In the **last few days**	31%	44%	13%	4%	2%	3%	2%
On **polling day / on the day I filled out my postal vote**	32%	39%	14%	5%	5%	2%	3%

■ Conservative ■ Labour ■ Liberal Democrat ■ SNP ■ UKIP ■ Green ■ Other

Lord Ashcroft Polls
🐦 @LordAshcroft

Thinking about the Conservative/Labour party election campaign, was it...

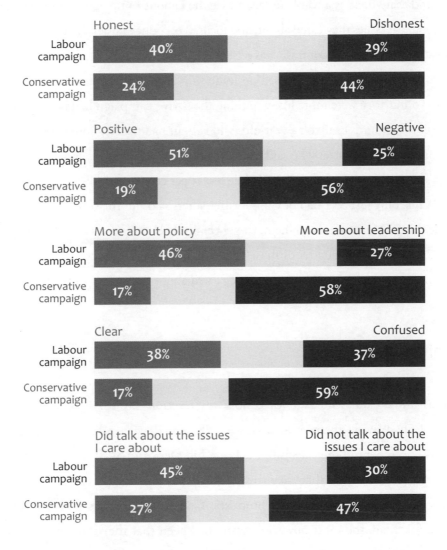

Honest | Dishonest
- Labour campaign: 40% | 29%
- Conservative campaign: 24% | 44%

Positive | Negative
- Labour campaign: 51% | 25%
- Conservative campaign: 19% | 56%

More about policy | More about leadership
- Labour campaign: 46% | 27%
- Conservative campaign: 17% | 58%

Clear | Confused
- Labour campaign: 38% | 37%
- Conservative campaign: 17% | 59%

Did talk about the issues I care about | Did not talk about the issues I care about
- Labour campaign: 45% | 30%
- Conservative campaign: 27% | 47%

Lord Ashcroft Polls
@LordAshcroft

In a further post-election survey of 20,000 voters, conducted in late June and early July, I found that voters as a whole tended to see the Labour campaign as positive, honest, talking about the issues they cared about, and focused on policy rather than leadership. The Conservative campaign, by contrast, was regarded as negative, dishonest, not talking about issues people cared about, and focused on leadership rather than policy; even those who ended up voting Tory were more likely to think the party's campaign had been "confused" than "clear". Two thirds of 18 to 24 year-olds said Labour had talked about issues they cared about (compared to a quarter who said the same of the Conservatives), and 71 per cent said the party's campaign had been positive (while just 13 per cent said this had been true of the Tories). While only just over half of Conservative voters said the Tory campaign had talked about the things that mattered to them, 84 per cent of Labour voters said the same of their party's campaign. Only a quarter of those who switched away from the Conservatives said their former party had talked about what they cared about during the campaign.

Motivations

As well as finding out who had voted how, my election-day survey also looked into why people had made their various choices. Presented with a list of reasons which might have been behind their decision, Labour, Lib Dem and SNP voters said the most important factor had been that they trusted the motives of the party they chose; next, that they had preferred that party's promises. Conservative voters had had different priorities: for them, the most powerful reason had been that they thought the party or its leader would do a better job of negotiating Brexit; this was followed by the belief that Theresa May was the best Prime Minister on offer.

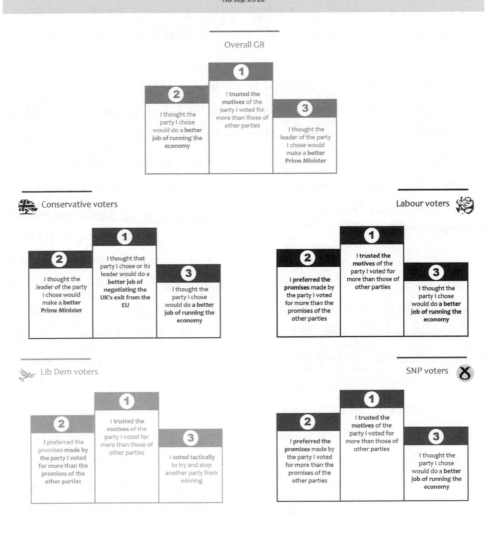

Here are some reasons people have given for deciding on the party they ended up voting for. Please can you rank them in order of how important they were in your decision, from first to third, even if there were other reasons that were important to you?

NB top three

Overall GB

1 I trusted the motives of the party I voted for more than those of other parties

2 I thought the party I chose would do a **better job of running the economy**

3 I thought the leader of the party I chose would make a **better Prime Minister**

Conservative voters

1 I thought that party I chose or its leader would do a **better job of negotiating the UK's exit from the EU**

2 I thought the leader of the party I chose would make a **better Prime Minister**

3 I thought the party I chose would do a **better job of running the economy**

Labour voters

1 I trusted the motives of the party I voted for more than those of other parties

2 I preferred the **promises** made by the party I voted for more than the promises of the other parties

3 I thought the party I chose would do a **better job of running the economy**

Lib Dem voters

1 I trusted the motives of the party I voted for more than those of other parties

2 I preferred the **promises** made by the party I voted for more than the promises of the other parties

3 I voted tactically to try and stop another party from winning

SNP voters

1 I trusted the motives of the party I voted for more than those of other parties

2 I preferred the **promises** made by the party I voted for more than the promises of the other parties

3 I thought the party I chose would do a **better job of running the economy**

Lord Ashcroft Polls
@LordAshcroft

Asked unprompted which issues had mattered most in their voting decision, Conservatives were most likely to name Brexit (as were Liberal Democrats), followed by having the right leadership. Labour voters, meanwhile, named the NHS and spending cuts above anything else; fewer than one in ten mentioned Brexit, compared to nearly half of those who voted Tory.

Our July post-election survey found that nearly one in ten of the 2017 Labour vote was made up of people who said they don't usually vote in elections, who had never previously done so or for whom this had been the first time they were eligible; this was the case for only three per cent of those who voted Conservative. Accordingly, there was a huge difference in voting behaviour depending on how regularly people said they turned out. Those who said they always vote at general elections no matter what divided 45 per cent to 39 per cent for the Conservatives, and those who said they usually vote split evenly, with 42 per cent for each of the two main parties. Those who said they do not usually vote at elections but did so this time went for Labour by 54 to 31 per cent; nearly three quarters of those who had never voted at a general election before even though they were eligible to do so went for Jeremy Corbyn's party. Those who were eligible to vote for the first time chose Labour over the Tories by more than two to one.

Those who do not usually vote, or had never previously voted despite having been eligible to do so, gave different reasons for turning out this time, depending on which party they had chosen. Those who had voted Tory were most likely to say they had particularly wanted to vote against one of the other parties or leaders, or that their vote was "because of Brexit" (the latter also being the most frequent explanation given by those who chose the Lib Dems). For Labour voters, though, the single most important reason given for turning out this time when they don't usually do so was that "a current party

Which was the most important issue when it came to deciding how to vote in the general election?

All voters

	Brexit	28%
	NHS	17%
	Economy / Jobs	8%
	The right leadership / the best PM	8%
	Immigration	6%

Conservative voters

	Brexit	48%
	The right leadership / the best PM	13%
	Economy / Jobs	11%
	Immigration	9%
	Terrorism / security	7%

Labour voters

	NHS	33%
	Spending cuts	11%
	Brexit	8%
	Poverty	7%
	Economy / Jobs	6%

Lib Dem voters

	Brexit	31%
	NHS	19%
	Economy / Jobs	7%
	Other	6%
	Spending cuts	5%

SNP voters

	Other	18%
	NHS	15%
	Brexit	13%
	Spending cuts	9%
	Poverty	8%

or leader has made me more enthusiastic". This just pipped voting against another party or leader; their third most popular reason was that they were "angry or upset about the state of the country".

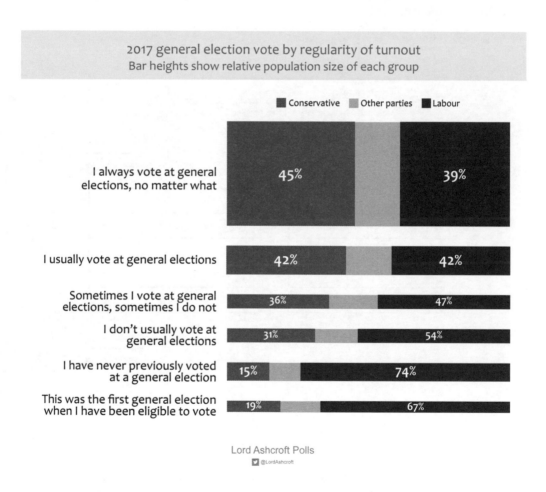

2017 general election vote by regularity of turnout
Bar heights show relative population size of each group

Lord Ashcroft Polls
@LordAshcroft

We also asked people what policies they could remember the two main parties putting forward during the election campaign. In the unprompted answers, the biggest single area on which they could recall hearing from the Conservatives was Brexit, mentioned by nearly one in three of those who could remember any policies at all. The second biggest area of recall was social care, or as many put it, the "Dementia Tax", mentioned by one in five of those who remembered anything. Being "strong and stable" was the third most often remembered Tory "policy", followed by the removal of the triple lock on pensions and the possible reintroduction of fox hunting.

In the previous question you said you don't usually vote at general elections. Why did you vote at this election?

Conservative voters

	To vote against one of the parties/leaders	32%
	Brexit	25%
	Have become more interested in politics recently	14%
	Angry or upset about the state of the country	7%
	A party/leader has made me more enthusiastic	5%

Labour voters

	A party/leader has made me more enthusiastic	25%
	To vote against one of the parties/leaders	23%
	Angry or upset about the state of the country	14%
	Have become more interested in politics recently	12%
	Brexit	6%

Liberal Democrat voters

	Brexit	28%
	To vote against one of the parties/leaders	20%
	Angry or upset about the state of the country	11%
	Have become more interested in politics recently	11%
	A party/leader has made me more enthusiastic	4%

Lord Ashcroft Polls
@LordAshcroft

Scrapping university tuition fees was the most remembered Labour policy among voters as a whole, mentioned by a quarter of those who recalled any policy and 15 per cent of all respondents. Younger voters were the most likely to mention it. Labour voters themselves were most likely to remember policies on the NHS; these were second among voters overall. "Spending too much" or "bankrupting the country" was third on the list of spontaneously recalled Labour plans, despite being mentioned almost exclusively by Conservative voters. Smaller numbers remembered Labour promises on tax, and the slogan of being "for the many not the few".

Only two per cent of respondents spontaneously said they remembered hearing Tory proposals on the NHS; only one per cent mentioned Labour policies on Brexit.

What, if anything, can you remember from the policies
the Conservatives/Labour offered at the general election?

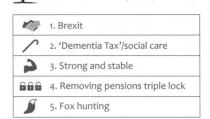

Conservative party

	1. Brexit
	2. 'Dementia Tax'/social care
	3. Strong and stable
	4. Removing pensions triple lock
	5. Fox hunting

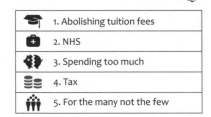

Labour party

	1. Abolishing tuition fees
	2. NHS
	3. Spending too much
	4. Tax
	5. For the many not the few

Lord Ashcroft Polls
@LordAshcroft

And now, the news

BBC television had been the most important news source for 40 per cent of Conservative voters – higher than for those of any other party, and above the average of one in three voters overall. Only 13 per cent of Tories said newspapers had been their main source of election news, though this was nearly twice the level for voters as a whole and nearly three times that of those who had voted Labour. Nearly one in five of Labour voters (and nearly a quarter of 18 to 24 year-olds) said their biggest source of political news during the campaign had been Facebook, Twitter, blogs or websites other than those of the BBC or newspapers; only six in a hundred Conservative voters said these had been their main sources.

Despite the huge sums the Conservative Party reportedly spent on Facebook advertising, most people said they did not remember seeing any of it. Nor did we find evidence that such advertising was successfully targeted – swing voters who switched to or from the Tories, or who considered voting for the party but decided against, were no more likely to recall seeing it than anybody else. Indeed, voters as a whole were slightly more likely to say they had seen paid adverts or promotions on social media from Labour than from the Conservatives.

But the real difference between the parties when it came to social media was not in paid-for content, but the impact of sharing. The proportion who said they had often seen pro-Labour items shared by other people they followed was more than double that which said the same of the Conservatives. Nearly seven in ten 18 to 24 year-olds said they had seen Labour-boosting material shared on social media, more than three times as many as had often seen content shared in support of the Tories.

Thinking about social media, how often do you recall seeing any stories
or adverts supporting the Conservative/Labour party...
By age

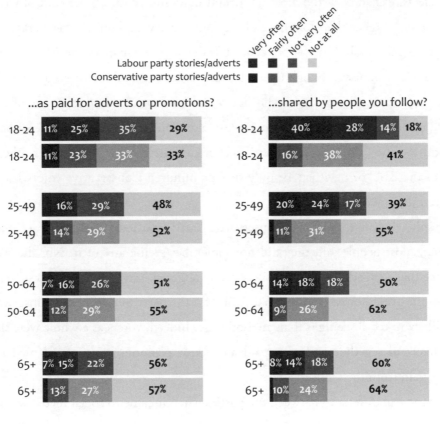

Labour party stories/adverts
Conservative party stories/adverts

Very often
Fairly often
Not very often
Not at all

...as paid for adverts or promotions?

18-24	11%	25%	35%	29%
18-24	11%	23%	33%	33%
25-49	16%	29%	48%
25-49	14%	29%	52%
50-64	7%	16%	26%	51%
50-64	12%	29%	55%
65+	7%	15%	22%	56%
65+	13%	27%	57%

...shared by people you follow?

18-24	40%	28%	14%	18%
18-24	16%	38%	41%
25-49	20%	24%	17%	39%
25-49	11%	31%	55%
50-64	14%	18%	18%	50%
50-64	9%	26%	62%
65+	8%	14%	18%	60%
65+	10%	24%	64%

Lord Ashcroft Polls
@LordAshcroft

An Inconvenient Youth

Where social class was once the great dividing line between Labour and Conservative voters, this has been superseded by age. Labour had a clear lead over the Tories among younger voters in 2015, but two years later the differential was dramatic: two thirds of 18 to 24 year-olds voted Labour, according to my election day post-vote survey, with fewer than one in five voting Conservative; Labour also won 58 per cent of 25 to 34s, compared to the Tories' 22 per cent. Labour even won by a 20-point margin among those aged 35 to 44.

Among those who voted Conservative in both 2015 and 2017, the median age was 61; among those switching to the Tories, it was 56; among those switching away, it was 45. The median age of people who did not vote Conservative in either election is 43.

Brexit was an important reason why the Tories did less well with younger voters in 2017. Not only were 2015 Tories who voted remain (who tended to be younger) more likely to switch away from the party than leavers, but younger remainers were more likely to move away than older remainers. In our survey, nearly four in ten 18 to 24 year-olds said they would still like to prevent Brexit from happening if at all possible; only 19 per cent said they supported leaving the EU, fewer than any other group apart from Liberal Democrat voters.

For 18 to 24s, though, improving the NHS was the most important issue facing both the country as a whole (with negotiating Brexit on the right terms in second place), and for themselves and their families (with the cost of living second; Brexit was fourth, with only a quarter naming it as a personal priority). They saw the Conservative Party's biggest priorities as Brexit, immigration and the deficit, while Labour's were the NHS, tackling poverty (which was named as one of the top issues facing the country by a quarter of them – six times the number of Tory voters who did so) and tackling the cost of living. This age group was five times as likely to say Britain was on the wrong track as to say it was heading in the right direction, making it much more pessimistic on this question than the population as a whole.

Voters under 24 were less likely than most – especially Conservatives – to say the BBC and other television news had been their main source of political information during the election campaign, and only three in a hundred said it had been newspapers. As we saw above, they were more likely than most voters to name the BBC website, and much more likely to name Twitter, Facebook and other websites or blogs.

In a series of focus groups I held after the election, first-time voters said they felt that Labour had made an effort to engage them, especially on social media, which for some had been their main or indeed only source of information ("the only way I got Labour's message"). The same could not be said of the Tories: "I don't follow politics really closely. In the channels I do follow, I barely remember seeing any Conservative campaigning, it was mostly Labour;" "I don't think the Conservatives tried hard enough to engage with students and get my attention." Pro-Labour content that people could remember included Jeremy Corbyn addressing crowds at public meetings or concerts, or talking to ordinary people, and several had seen material about fox hunting ("mainly because I have lots of vegan friends on social media"). The balance had mostly been positive rather than anti-Conservative (although "the Tories made themselves very easy to demonise"), and much of that had been light-hearted: "entertaining stuff like wheat field memes", after the PM had revealed in an interview that running through wheat fields had been the naughtiest thing she had done as a child.

"You very much got the impression that Jeremy Corbyn was going out, meeting people, getting to the heart of what people really want."

For most of these voters, however, there was more to the appeal of Labour's campaign than its presence on social media. A large part of its attraction had been that the party, and Jeremy Corbyn in particular, seemed to be talking and listening to real people. While the Tories seemed "cold" and "distant" (they refused to take part in debates and "were only interested in holding rallies for party members"), Labour seemed "grounded in the community": "You very much got the impression that Jeremy Corbyn was going out, meeting people, getting to the heart of what people really want"; "I also saw lots of videos of him just chatting to regular people while canvassing… to see him just comfortably talking with normal people, especially in comparison to Theresa May, resonated with me"; "I attended an open-air talk by Corbyn in York that anyone could go to, and it just felt like a properly popular movement". The PM, meanwhile, had sounded "quite naggy – she kept droning on the same message and it made me switch off".

"I work for the NHS, commute on public transport, have large student debts and can't afford a house – I think I'm Labour's ideal target voter."

The tone of Labour's campaign – "hopeful", "motivational and positive" – had also played an important part. "It was about making Britain great again, whereas May's campaign was very serious and there was a lot of scaremongering". Labour "gave lots of people a reason to believe life could be better". Though much of what the party had to say was about ending austerity, "the overall message was a message of hope, that another fairer society is possible". Specific policies, including abolishing university tuition fees, also mattered: "As soon as I saw that Labour wanted to abolish university fees I pretty much made up my mind. It made me think they were listening to my generation and wanted to put us first;" "I work for the NHS, commute on public transport, have large student debts and can't afford a house – I think I'm Labour's ideal target voter;" "I was reluctant at first because I was sceptical about Corbyn. But I thought it was an incredibly positive campaign. My life would be transformed if I could leave uni in no debt. I was genuinely excited by the prospect of a Labour government by the end." The Conservatives, meanwhile, "seemed to think people were obligated to vote for them because May said she needed a mandate for Brexit."

A few had been tempted by the Liberal Democrats, "the only party willing to renege on Brexit", but "they didn't have any realistic chance of winning and I have not forgotten their tuition fees betrayal… How can we be sure they won't break their promises again?" It was also unclear what else the party stood for – apart from their policy on Europe, all most of our participants had heard about them was "Farron's stance on gay people".

Asked in our survey about their preferred Prime Minister, 60 per cent of the youngest voters favoured Jeremy Corbyn, compared to just 17 per cent for Theresa May; a quarter were not sure. Less than one in six in this age group said they thought the Conservative Party was on the side of people like them, wanted to help ordinary people get on in life, shared their values, would do what it said it would do, represented the whole country not just some types of people, stood for fairness or opportunity for all, or was united. While 44 per cent said they thought the Tories had a vision for the future of the country, two thirds said this was true of Labour – and similar proportions also said Jeremy Corbyn's party stood for fairness and opportunity and had its heart in the right place, and nearly three quarters said it wanted to help ordinary people get on in life.

For those aged 24 and under who said they did not usually vote at general elections (and our survey found that more than a quarter of 2017 Labour voters did not vote in 2010), the biggest reasons for having turned out this time were that they had become more interested in politics in recent years, followed closely by the claim that a current party or leader had made them more enthusiastic. Majorities in this group said the Labour campaign had been honest, clear, focused on policy rather than leadership, talked about issues they cared about and (most of all) had been positive. Majorities said the opposite had been true of the Conservative campaign in every case. Of those who had not voted Conservative at the election, only one in five said they could imagine doing so in the future; more than half said they could never see themselves voting Tory.

The Brexit election?

From the time Theresa May sprang her April surprise it was clear that this was to be, at least as far as the Tories were concerned, the Brexit election. The Prime Minister was betting that by asking directly for a mandate to negotiate Britain's EU departure she would attract large numbers of leave voters who had not supported the Conservatives in 2015 (especially from Labour, on a big enough scale to turn a substantial number of seats from red to blue) and that, crucially, she would do so while holding on to the great majority of Tories from the previous election, including those who voted remain in the referendum.

There is no doubt that Brexit was a major part of the Conservatives' appeal, especially to those who had not voted for the party the last time round. As Matthew Goodwin and Oliver Heath demonstrated in detail in their paper *The 2017 General Election, Brexit and the Return to Two-Party Politics: An Aggregate-Level Analysis of the Result*, the Tories were most likely to improve their showing in areas that voted to leave the EU. In the 20 most pro-Brexit constituencies the Conservative vote share rose by an average of 15 points, nearly three times the national rate. As our own post-election survey found, of those who voted Tory in 2017 having not done so two years earlier, three quarters had voted leave in the referendum. And as our focus groups had found during the campaign, Brexit was the issue most likely to persuade previous non-Tories to see this election in a different light. As we saw above, our election-day post-vote poll found Conservative voters saying the biggest reason for their decision had been choosing the best leader or party to negotiate Brexit – and those for whom that had been the main issue at stake overwhelmingly backed the Tories. Yet the fact that the Conservatives ended up with fewer seats than they started with is evidence enough that the Prime Minister's bet did not pay off. If this was the Brexit election, what went wrong?

One reason for the Tories' miscalculation is that Brexit was just not important enough to enough people. Negotiating Britain's exit from the EU on the right terms was named more often than anything else as the single most important issue facing the country – but even then, only by 29 per cent of voters. It was mentioned among the top three issues by half of all voters, but on this score it was outstripped by the NHS – especially on the question of what mattered to "me and my family", where Brexit fell into third place behind tackling the cost of living.

Another is that the people most likely to put Brexit at the top of the national agenda were highly likely to be Tories already. Only one in five voters thought both that negotiating Britain's EU departure was a top-three issue *and* that the Conservatives best represented their view of how the country should handle the matter – and of these, 63 per cent had voted Conservative at the previous election. At the same time, those who had voted Tory in 2015 were nearly twice as likely as those who had voted Labour to consider EU negotiations the country's top priority. (A similar dynamic, incidentally, helps to explain why the Liberal Democrats did not have more success in turning Brexit

Top 5 issue priorities by 2015 general election + EU referendum vote

Issues seen as one of the three biggest priorities...

● for me and my family   ● facing Britain as a whole

Conservative Leave voters

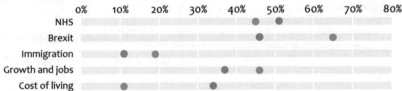

Conservative Remain voters

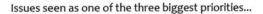

Labour Leave voters

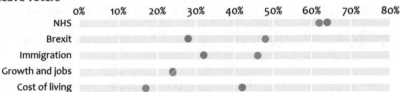

Labour Remain voters

Lord Ashcroft Polls
🐦 @LordAshcroft

to their advantage. Only just over half of those who voted remain said they would still like to prevent Britain's EU departure if at all possible, and only one in three of these Brexit "resisters" thought the Lib Dems were best placed to handle the negotiations; they were slightly more likely to name Labour.)

A further, related, explanation is that previous Labour supporters who had voted leave in the referendum were much more hesitant about the idea of voting Conservative than the Tories might have expected. This is partly because, though they supported Brexit, other things mattered to them more: the issue was second to the NHS on the question of priorities for the country, and fourth behind the NHS, the cost of living and immigration for themselves and their families.

Our post-election focus groups with these "Labour Leavers" who had stayed with their party in 2017 confirmed that Brexit was by no means the only issue on the agenda. "A general election is about everything," said one, but the Tories "barely acknowledged that there are other issues that need addressing". While "Labour did the broader 'home' policies" – the NHS, helping "the majority not the few", social housing, public sector pay – "the Tories stuck to Brexit. For them it was a one-policy election."

"Jezza wants to make sure people in this country are protected."

Also, thinking Brexit was important was one thing; thinking the Conservatives were the best party to deal with it was quite another. The Tory campaign was "trying to convince us that Mrs. May's approach was the only way", but Labour "would be able to negotiate a better deal for the ordinary people" rather than "corporate business", which would be the Conservative priority. Some had voted leave in the hope that they would see "more money spent on schools and the NHS", which was also Labour's plan. Jeremy Corbyn would also be "less confrontational" and thus more effective, and would want a deal that would "protect jobs and workers' rights": "Jezza wants to make sure people in this country are protected."

Though they had been impressed that "Jeremy Corbyn suddenly seemed to develop a personality" during the campaign, some still had reservations about voting for the party. However, these had mostly been to do with his stance on defence: none said the party's approach to Brexit had been a hurdle for them. In the end, most had voted Labour more enthusiastically at this election than in 2017 – not least because the Tories had given the impression of thinking "we've got this in the bag" – and now thought more highly of both their party and its leader than they had before the campaign.

As with "Labour Leavers", there was some expectation that the Conservatives would do well among people who had voted Labour some years ago but switched to UKIP in 2015 – that the socially conservative, pro-Brexit party would act as a "gateway drug" for the Tories. In the event, the smaller party ended up giving roughly the same number of voters back to Labour as it had taken from them in the first place.

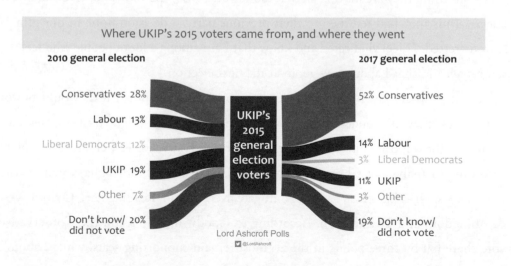

Where UKIP's 2015 voters came from, and where they went

2010 general election

Conservatives 28%
Labour 13%
Liberal Democrats 12%
UKIP 19%
Other 7%
Don't know/ 20%
did not vote

UKIP's 2015 general election voters

2017 general election

52% Conservatives
14% Labour
3% Liberal Democrats
11% UKIP
3% Other
19% Don't know/ did not vote

Lord Ashcroft Polls
@LordAshcroft

In our focus groups, people who had gone from Labour to UKIP in 2015 said they had made the switch because of immigration, Europe, the feeling that Nigel Farage was in touch with people, and that the party "showed the unrest the people of Britain are feeling – hence the Brexit result". At the start of the 2017 campaign most had been unsure how they would end up voting: UKIP had "lost their momentum" since the referendum ("I never heard anything about them this time, I didn't even know they were standing"), and "since Nigel Farage left it has gone to pot". But these voters were more sceptical than our "Labour Leavers" about Jeremy Corbyn and Labour, and gave a higher priority to the Brexit negotiations as an election issue. However, some were confused that Theresa May "never explained what she had in mind for Brexit", frustrated that "it's taking too long" and even worried that "the Tories want to delay it as much as they can". Labour had not been any clearer on the subject "but overall it was a more compassionate and caring manifesto", while the Conservatives were proposing "more cuts", the "nasty Dementia Tax and winter warmer payments cut", and "HS2, that train thing they are wasting all that money on". Also, "pensions was a complete car crash". Thus they had returned to their previous party, a decision none in our groups now regretted: "I feel vindicated and know that I am among a lot of people who feel the same way, and that Labour may get in at the next election."

If the Conservatives misjudged how much of an attraction Brexit would be for non-Tories, they also underestimated the extent to which it might push former supporters in the opposite direction. Many of the Conservative losses were in seats which, according to analysis by Chris Hanretty of the University of East Anglia, voted heavily to remain, such as Battersea, Enfield Southgate, Kensington, Reading East, Oxford West & Abingdon, and Twickenham. According to Goodwin and Heath, the Conservative vote share fell by three points in the 20 most remain-supporting seats, while Labour's rose by 13 points. This meant that the Tory–Labour swing in heavily remain areas was bigger than the Labour–Tory swing in places that voted most strongly to leave.

Again, our post-election poll adds to the picture. While 86 per cent of 2015 Conservatives who voted leave in the referendum supported the party again in 2017, only 68 per cent of 2015 Tory Remainers did so. Those who switched away from the Conservatives were twice as likely to have voted remain than those who stayed. Remainers who voted Tory in 2015 were twice as likely to defect from the party if they were aged under 50, and even more likely to do so if they were still resistant to Brexit – that is, if they said they still wanted to prevent it from happening, rather than that the people had chosen to leave and the government must carry out their wishes. Moreover, those who moved away from the Conservatives having voted to remain in the EU were more likely than leave voters to switch to another party, rather than simply stay at home. While 18 per cent of "Labour Leavers" switched to the Conservatives and only 15 per cent of "Tory Remainers" went to Labour, the second group was bigger than the first, meaning the overall net movement was in Labour's favour.

Finally, while Conservative fortunes in any given area were closely tied to how that area had voted in the referendum, the same was not true of Labour to anything like the same extent. While the Tory vote share rose by more than average in the most pro-Brexit areas and fell in the most pro-remain, Labour's rose across the board. Though Labour's increase was slightly lower in heavily leave-voting areas than elsewhere, their general advance was enough to blunt the swing to the Conservatives, allowing them to hold on to seats they would otherwise have lost (and sometimes by the skin of their teeth: in Dudley North, one of the most pro-Brexit constituencies in the country, Labour managed to grow their share in the face of a 15-point Tory surge and keep the seat by 22 votes). Nor were changes in Labour's vote share as closely related as changes in the Conservatives' to demographic factors, like the number of graduates in an area, or its ethnic minority population. And as our post-election survey found, only a quarter of Labour voters named the EU negotiations as one of the most important issues to them and their families. For millions of people, in other words, this was not the Brexit election at all.

4 / Where are we now?

FOUR DAYS AFTER the general election, Theresa May appeared before the 1922 Committee of Conservative backbenchers. "I got us into this mess, I'll get us out of it," she told them. Accepting responsibility for the election gamble and its consequences, she said she would serve as Prime Minister "as long as you want me", an acknowledgment that her future was in their hands. "She pitched it spot on," one MP present is reported to have said.

The threat of an immediate leadership challenge receded, but the weeks that followed offered no respite. A fortnight after her 1922 appearance the Conservatives finally concluded a "confidence and supply" arrangement in which Northern Ireland's Democratic Unionist Party guaranteed that its ten MPs would vote with the government on the Queen's Speech, the Budget, and any legislation on Brexit and national security. The deal included an extra £1 billion in public spending in the province, prompting political opponents to ask where the PM had suddenly found the "magic money tree" she had previously said would be needed to satisfy other parties' plans. With no majority to see them through, the government quietly dropped controversial manifesto policies from its legislative programme, including new grammar schools, the scrapping of free school meals and the social care reforms that helped torpedo the Tory campaign. A series of leaks exposed high-level disagreements over issues including Brexit negotiating objectives and public sector pay. Labour crept ahead in most published polls, which also showed Theresa May and Jeremy Corbyn all but tied on the question of who would make the best PM.

As Westminster came to terms with the new dispensation, my research looked in detail at how people saw things in the aftermath of the unexpected result.

No regrets

My 20,000-sample post-election survey found most voters, including most Labour voters, and a majority of those switching away from the Conservatives, said they had expected the Tories to win – indeed, one in five of those who voted Labour had anticipated a big Conservative victory. Even so, few had any regrets about their decision, despite the unforeseen outcome. Only four in a hundred Tory voters – and only two in a hundred Labour voters – said they would choose a different party if they had the chance to go back and vote again. (One in ten Liberal Democrats said this; most of them said they would vote Labour if they could go back to 8th June).

> *"I think a little dose of humility has made Theresa May focus*
> *a bit more on trying to appeal to the electorate."*

In our post-election focus groups of those who had thought about voting Conservative but decided against, none said they would have done so after all had they known how close the result would be. If anything, some thought, the voters' verdict might have taught the Tories a lesson: "I think they'd be a lot more arrogant if they had a majority. Being in this position makes them consider their policies more carefully;" "I also think a little dose of humility has made Theresa May focus a bit more on trying to appeal to the electorate." Inescapably, though, the result only added to the uncertainty over Brexit and the economy, leaving some with a sense of unease: "We still seem to be in a state of limbo, and to be quite honest, it doesn't feel right."

We found fewer than three in ten voters saying they thought Britain was heading in the right direction, with nearly half disagreeing. Not surprisingly, there were differences according to party affiliation, but this was not just a partisan question: more than one in three of those who had voted Conservative thought things were going in the wrong direction. Nor was it simply a matter of the individual's view of Brexit: though leavers were five times as likely as remainers to say the country was on the right track, that still amounted to only just over half of them; more than one in five of those who had voted to leave the EU nevertheless thought Britain was heading the wrong way.

Labour and the Tories: What are they like…?

Nearly half of all respondents in my post-election survey said their view of the Conservative Party had become less favourable since the election – eight times as many as said the opposite. Those whose opinion of the party had declined included more than one in four who had voted for it, and Tories who had voted to stay in the EU were more likely to say this than those who had voted to leave. Meanwhile, slightly more said Labour had risen in their estimations than fallen.

We asked those who had voted Conservative but said their opinion of the party had become less favourable since the election to say why this was so. Among the unprompted answers, by far the biggest category concerned Theresa May and the general leadership they thought the party was offering (or failing to offer), with many more commenting that the Tories seemed weak, indecisive, or even incompetent and shambolic. The next biggest grumble was the government's deal with the DUP, including the complaint that the Prime Minister had found a billion pounds to appease her new partners despite telling public sector workers there was no "magic money tree". This was followed by the impression of infighting and "bickering" between Conservatives. The idea that the party had called a needless election and taken voters for granted also featured prominently. A large number mentioned the EU – but as many grumbled that the Tories were pursuing a "hard Brexit" as protested that they were "not going through with Brexit".

Our survey looked in more detail at how people saw the two main parties following the general election campaign. We asked people whether they associated fifteen positive characteristics with Labour and the Conservatives (it was possible, though rare, for people to say that any of them applied to both).

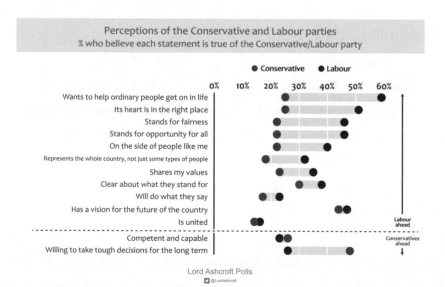

Perceptions of the Conservative and Labour parties
% who believe each statement is true of the Conservative/Labour party

● Conservative   ● Labour

Lord Ashcroft Polls
@LordAshcroft

Our 20,000 respondents were more likely to say an attribute was true of the Tories than Labour in only two cases: being willing to take tough decisions for the long term, and being competent and capable. On the first of these, the Conservatives led by a 22-point margin, a similar result to those I found on the same question during the previous election in 2015. But on competence, the Tory advantage was a mere three points – indeed only just over a quarter of voters said "competent and capable" was a true description of the party. A year earlier, shortly after the EU referendum, I had found 41 per cent saying competence was one of the Tories' features.

This meant the Conservatives were doing little better in a traditional area of strength than they were on measures on which they had historically been on the back foot. No more than one in four voters thought the party was on the side of people like them, stood for fairness, or had its "heart in the right place". On these qualities, and others that explored the parties' values and motivations, Labour's already clear lead had doubled compared to my research from two years earlier.

In the poll we also asked people for the first word or phrase that came to mind when they thought of each of the main parties. The answers are reproduced in the word clouds below (though some have had to be removed, this being a family publication). Most positive comments about the Conservatives concerned strength, stability, toughness or realism, but many more of the associations were negative, often relating to wealth, class or dishonesty. "Rich", "strong", "liars" and "nasty" were the most commonly used words, all of which were unprompted.

Answers for Labour suggested a more benevolent view of the party's intentions, with "fair" or "fairness" appearing more often than any other words. The idea that the party was caring, was for the many not the few, and represented the working class also featured prominently. Negative associations usually concerned competence, especially on tax and spending, and the suggestion that the party was too left wing. The words our participants most often said came to mind when thinking of the Liberal Democrats were "weak" and "nothing".

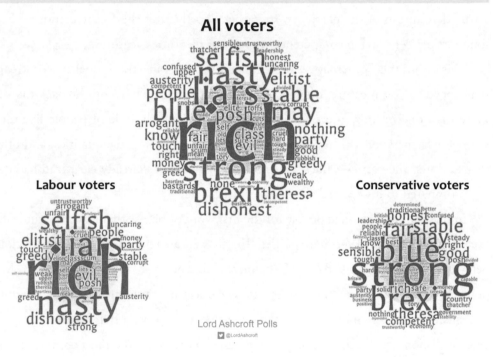

Lord Ashcroft Polls
@LordAshcroft

What is the first word or phrase that comes to mind
when you think of the Labour Party?

All voters

Labour voters

Conservative voters

Lord Ashcroft Polls
@LordAshcroft

What is the first word or phrase that comes to mind
when you think of the Liberal Democrats?

All voters

Lib Dem voters

Lord Ashcroft Polls
@LordAshcroft

Just over half of those who did not vote Conservative in 2017 said they could not imagine themselves ever doing so in the future. Among those who voted Labour, the proportion saying they could never see themselves voting Tory rose to three quarters. Of those who voted Conservative in 2015 but did not do so this time, only just over half said they could see themselves returning to the party.

Those who had not voted Labour were more open to the idea of switching to the party in future than non-Tories were about the Conservatives. Three quarters of Labour voters said they ruled out ever voting Tory, while only two thirds of those who had voted Conservative said they could never see themselves switching to Labour. More than twice as many Lib Dem voters said they could imagine switching to Labour as to the Conservatives.

…And what do they want?

We asked people to tell us their biggest fear about a Labour or a Conservative government with an overall majority. For respondents as a whole and those who had voted Labour, the biggest fears of another Tory majority concerned the NHS, followed by the prospect of more cuts, and the consequences of Brexit. Worries about a Labour government were heavily concentrated around the economy, particularly the possibility of excessive spending and debt, and the prospect of Jeremy Corbyn being in charge.

To understand more about how they saw the parties' agendas, we asked people which of fourteen issues were the most important facing Britain as whole, and which mattered most to themselves and their families. We then asked which they thought were the biggest priorities for the Conservative Party and for Labour.

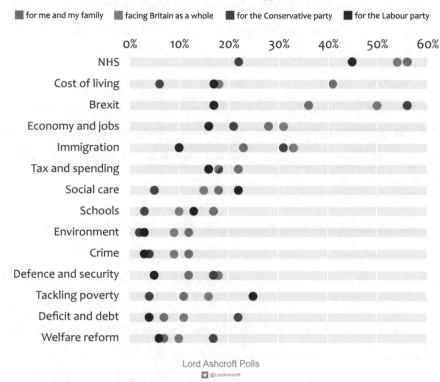

Lord Ashcroft Polls
@LordAshcroft

Different kinds of voters had different agendas, as we will see in more detail later on. But looking at the electorate as a whole, there are some clear patterns when we compare what matters to them, what they say matters to the country, and what they think matters to the parties.

Negotiating Britain's EU exit on the right terms was selected most often as the single most important issue, albeit by only 29 per cent of respondents. But when we look at the top three choices it falls slightly behind the NHS, which was named in the top three by a majority of all voters. When asked what mattered most to themselves and their families, there was a 20-point gap between the NHS and Brexit (indeed the NHS was picked most often as the single biggest priority on this score), and tackling the cost of living rose to second place overall.

The NHS, jobs, the cost of living, tackling poverty, social care, schools, crime and the environment were more likely to be chosen as important issues for the country than to be thought priorities for the Conservative Party – while people were more likely to think Brexit, the deficit and the debt, and welfare reform were priorities for the Tories than to say they were among the top three issues for Britain as a whole.

A further pattern that emerged was that nearly all the things thought more likely to matter to the Conservatives than Labour were also named more often as issues facing the country than to individuals and their families (economic growth and jobs, welfare reform, defence and security, the deficit and the debt, immigration and Brexit). By the same token, nearly all the questions believed to exercise Labour more than the Tories were also named more often as priorities for "me and my family" than for Britain as whole (the cost of living, schools, social care and the NHS).

One of the striking things about the findings of this research, and of the campaign itself, is the retreat of the deficit and the debt as an election issue. My election day poll in 2015 found more than half of Conservative voters naming "cutting the deficit and the debt" as one of the most important issues facing the country – second only to "getting the economy growing and creating jobs". Only 17 per cent of Tories said they thought it a priority in my 2017 post-election survey, and it ranked tenth for voters overall, behind defence and security, tackling poverty, and improving social care. As we saw above, only just over one in five named the deficit as a high priority for the Conservatives – yet even this was twice as many as said it was a top-three issue for the country and three times the number who said it mattered to them and their families.

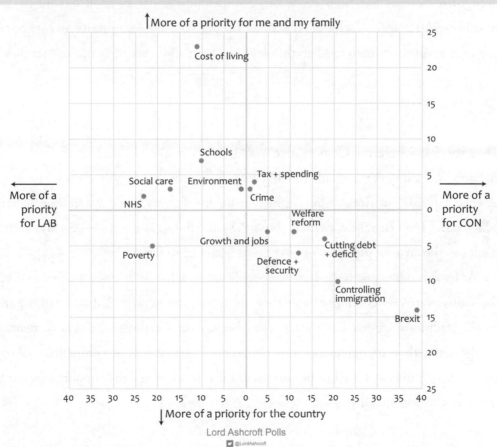

Issue priorities
Issues seen as one of the three biggest priorities for:
the country as a whole, me and my family, the Conservative party, the Labour party

Lord Ashcroft Polls
@LordAshcroft

Given the descent of the issue on the public agenda, it is perhaps not surprising that support has also fallen for the measures needed to tackle it. On election day two years ago, 84 per cent of Conservatives and 46 per cent of voters overall agreed that austerity needed to continue; after this election, only half of Tories and a quarter of voters overall agreed. Another quarter (including one in three who voted Conservative) said they thought some cuts had been needed to get spending under control, but no longer. Another quarter again (including half of all Labour voters) said austerity and spending cuts had never really been needed, they had just been an excuse to cut public services.

*   *   *

This, then, is where the Conservative brand stands in the wake of the 2017 general election. The campaign and subsequent events have hurt the party in areas where it has often struggled. The Tories now lag further behind Labour when voters think about which party is on their side, or cares about the same things as them – especially when it comes to the areas of policy whose impact feels closest to home.

At least as damaging is the fact that people are now hardly any more likely to think the Conservatives are competent as they are to say the same of Labour. For a party whose traditional appeal has always relied heavily on a claim to be able to manage things better than its opponents, this represents a serious loss of competitive advantage. It is one that will need to be corrected if it is to win back the support it needs to rediscover its lost majority.

5 / The new Conservative coalition

WINNING ELECTIONS MEANS building coalitions. Parties need supporters from the widest possible range of backgrounds, incomes, regions, classes, occupations, outlooks and levels of educational attainment if they hope to be elected to govern the whole country. If this seems an obvious point, it is even more true in the light of the 2017 election, when Labour and the Conservatives between them accounted for more than 82 per cent of the vote – the highest combined total for the two main parties since 1970. The next coalition of voters that produces a parliamentary majority for one party or the other will probably have to be bigger and broader than anything we have seen in a British election for decades.

To help understand the Conservative Party's challenge in creating such a movement we can examine the coalition of voters it managed to assemble at the 2017 election, and how it differed from the one it put together two years earlier. That means looking in detail at four groups of people. First, those who voted Tory in both elections; second, those who voted for the party in 2017 having not done so in 2015; third, those who voted Conservative in 2015 but not in 2017; and fourth, those who intended to back the Tories at some point in the campaign (helping to boost the party's early poll leads), but ultimately decided not to. We can call these four groups Loyalists, Joiners, Defectors and Considerers. My 20,000-sample post-election survey shows who they are, their political priorities, how they see issues like

Brexit and austerity, their views of the different parties, and their wider social attitudes. As well as defining who the Tories are holding, attracting and losing, it reveals some of the tensions in keeping their supporters together and expanding their numbers.

What separates Loyalists from Defectors?

First of all, our research shows the most important reasons why people found themselves in one of these four groups. Regression analysis of the data from our survey allows us to identify the most important factors separating 2015 Conservative voters who turned out for the party again two years later, and those who did not – in other words, what were the biggest things that drove Defectors to defect?

What separates Loyalists from Defectors? Top 10 most powerful factors	
1	Whether Conservatives most closely represent their views on Brexit
2	Social attitudes
3	Age
4	Whether austerity is still necessary
5	Whether negotiating Brexit on the right terms is a priority for the Conservative Party
6	Whether capitalism is a force for good
7	Whether the deficit and the debt are among the most important issues facing Britain
8	Whether tackling the cost of living is an important issue for you and your family
9	EU referendum vote
10	Whether defence and security is a priority for the Conservative Party

Even after accounting for demographic factors like social grade, by far the most powerful dynamic at play among those who had voted Conservative at the previous election was whether or not they felt the Tories most closely represented their view of how the UK should handle Brexit and what our relationship with the EU should be like once we leave: those who did not were significantly more likely to move away from the party.

Next was their wider social attitudes, or their degree of what we might call cosmopolitanism. Previous Tory voters who felt more positively towards immigration, multiculturalism and social liberalism were more likely to defect; those who felt more negatively about these things were more inclined to remain with the Conservatives.

Age was the third most important determinant of whether a 2015 Tory would stay or go. Even assuming all other things were equal – social background or political outlook – younger voters were significantly more likely to defect from the Conservative Party than older people.

The analysis picked up other important drivers. People who voted Conservative in 2015 and thought austerity was still necessary, that negotiating Brexit on the right terms was an important priority for the Tories, that capitalism was a force for good, that the deficit and the debt were among the most important issues facing Britain, as well as those who did not mention the cost of living among priorities for themselves and their families, or who voted to leave the EU, were significantly more likely to stay with the party in 2017 than those who thought the opposite in each case. Notably, three of the top ten most powerful drivers in this decision were related to Brexit.

Stay at home or switch parties?

Not all of those who defected from the Conservatives at the 2017 election ended up voting for another party: 36 per cent of them decided not to vote at all. Our regression analysis shows the most important differences between those who joined another camp, and those who simply stayed at home.

What separates Defectors who stayed at home from those who switched parties? Top 5 most powerful factors	
1	Whether Conservatives most closely represent their views on Brexit
2	EU referendum vote
3	Social attitudes
4	Whether austerity is still necessary
5	Whether capitalism is a force for good

Again, Brexit-related factors are among the most important. Defectors who nevertheless thought the Conservatives best represented their view on Brexit, or who voted leave in the EU referendum, were significantly more likely not to vote at all, while those who took a different view in either case were more likely to vote for another party instead.

The third most powerful distinguishing factor was whether they had "cosmopolitan" social attitudes (Defectors with more positive views of multiculturalism, immigration and social liberalism were more likely to switch parties rather than stay at home), their view of further austerity (those who thought it unnecessary were more likely to switch), and their view of capitalism (Defectors who thought it was a force for good were more likely to stay at home rather than back a different party).

What separates Conservative Joiners from those who stayed away?

As with Conservative Defectors, three of the top ten most powerful factors in attracting new voters to the Tories were related to Brexit. The best predictor of whether someone who did not vote Conservative in 2015 would do so in 2017 was whether or not they felt the party best represented their view of how to handle Brexit and the country's subsequent relationship with the EU. Second was the extent of their "cosmopolitan" social attitudes: those who were more positive about multiculturalism, immigration and social liberalism were significantly less likely to be attracted to the party, other things being equal.

What separates Joiners from persistent non-Conservatives? Top 10 most powerful factors	
1	Whether Conservatives most closely represent their views on Brexit
2	Social attitudes
3	Whether austerity is still necessary
4	EU referendum vote
5	Whether negotiating Brexit on the right terms is a priority for the Conservative Party
6	Whether improving the NHS is among the most important issues facing Britain
7	Whether capitalism is a force for good
8	Whether protecting the environment is among the most important issues facing Britain
9	Whether tackling poverty is among the most important issues facing Britain
10	Whether tackling poverty is among the most important issues facing me and my family

Previous non-Tories who voted leave in the referendum, thought negotiating Brexit on the right terms for Britain was a priority for the Tories, or thought capitalism was a force for good were significantly more likely to vote Conservative in 2017 than those who did not; those who thought improving the NHS, protecting the environment or tackling poverty were among the most important issues facing the country were significantly more likely to stay away from the party.

* * *

Finally, our research allows us to paint a detailed portrait of each of these crucial groups of voters – which will either have to be attracted into the Conservative voting coalition, or kept there, for the party to win the next general election, whenever it comes.

Conservative Loyalists

Conservative Loyalists voted for the party in both the 2015 and 2017 general elections. More than nine in ten of them were sure or fairly confident how they would vote from the beginning of the campaign, and 85 per cent said they always voted at general elections (compared to 55 per cent of the electorate as a whole), the highest of any political or demographic group.

Loyalists' median age is 61. They are more likely than the population as a whole to be in the AB social group (senior managers and professionals), and to live in the South East, the South West, and the East of England. They are less likely than average to have a degree. More than six in ten are married – a higher proportion than any other voter group – and they are nearly twice as likely to be retired (44 per cent) as the general population. More than eight in ten own their own home, including more than half who own it outright with no mortgage (compared to one in three voters overall). Loyalists put themselves further to the right on the political scale than any other group, including those who voted for UKIP in 2015 or 2017; more than half describe themselves as "slightly right of centre" or "fairly right-wing", compared to one in five of the general population. They are more likely to say they are highly politically engaged than the electorate as a whole and other Conservative voters, though less so than Labour and Liberal Democrat voters.

In the 2016 referendum, Loyalists voted to leave the EU by two to one. Nearly eight in ten say the Tories best represent their view of how the UK should handle Brexit; the remainder are more likely to mention UKIP than Labour or the Liberal Democrats.

Loyalists are slightly more likely than Conservative voters as a whole (but slightly less likely than Labour voters) to say they are happy with the decision they made at the election. Seven in ten Loyalists say the Conservative Party shares their values, and nearly two thirds say it stands for fairness, but only just over a quarter say the party is united.

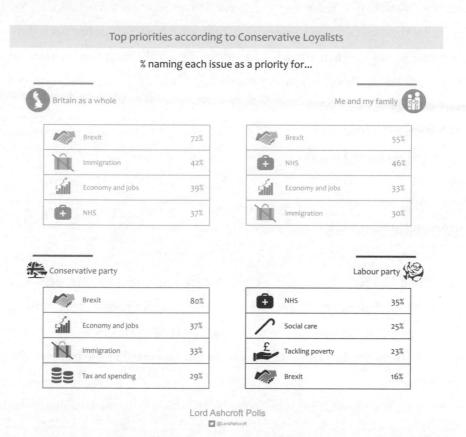

Lord Ashcroft Polls
@LordAshcroft

Conservative Loyalists name negotiating Brexit on the right terms as the most important issue both for the Britain as a whole and for themselves and their families. For the country, their second biggest priority is immigration; for themselves it is the NHS. Most Loyalists say continued austerity is needed to tackle the deficit and the debt (more than twice as many as among voters as a whole); one in three say cuts were necessary but austerity is no longer needed.

Nearly nine in ten Loyalists (compared to just over half of voters overall) agree that if you work hard it is possible to be very successful in Britain whatever your background; by three to two that life for most children growing up in Britain today will be better than it was for their parents (overall, six in ten think the opposite); and seven in ten think life in Britain today is better than it was thirty years ago (while a small majority of voters overall think it is worse). Loyalists are less likely than the population as a whole to see multiculturalism, social liberalism, feminism, the green movement and immigration as forces for good.

Conservative Joiners

Joiners voted Conservative in 2017 despite not having done so at the previous general election. Nearly half of them voted UKIP in 2015, around one in seven voted Labour, and eight per cent for the Lib Dems. More than half said they were sure how they would vote from the beginning of the campaign, and another quarter said they were fairly confident.

The median age of a Conservative Joiner is 56. They are disproportionately male, less likely than average to be in the AB and C1 (junior managerial and professional) social groups, more likely to be in the C2 (skilled manual worker) group, and much more likely than both Conservative Loyalists and Defectors to be in social group DE (semi-skilled, unskilled, and unemployed). They are much less likely than the population as a whole to have a degree. Conservative Joiners are more likely than average (though less likely than Loyalists) to be married, to be retired, and to own their own home. They are twice as likely as Loyalists to rent from a local authority or housing association, which they do at the same rate as the general population. Joiners put themselves to the right of the electorate as a whole, but are less likely to describe themselves as right-wing or right of centre than Conservative Loyalists.

Joiners are slightly less happy than Loyalists with their voting decision at the election: six per cent said they would go back and choose another party if they could, and half of those said they would vote Labour instead.

Three quarters of all Joiners – and 84 per cent of those who turned out – voted leave in the EU referendum. More than half say the Conservatives best represent their view of how the UK should handle Brexit, and a further one in four name UKIP. They are more enthusiastic about Brexit than Conservative Loyalists, and only five per cent say they would like to stop it happening (compared to 28 per cent of voters as a whole).

Joiners name Brexit as the most important issue both for Britain as a whole (with immigration second and the NHS third) and, by a smaller margin, for themselves and their families (with the NHS second and immigration third). Fewer than half – but nearly twice as many as among voters as a whole – think austerity is still needed; they are just as likely to think either that austerity is no longer necessary, or was never needed in the first place.

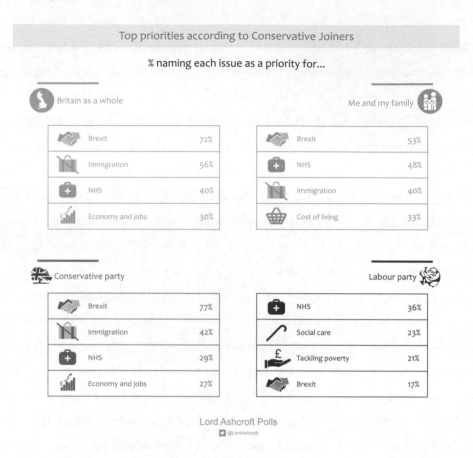

Top priorities according to Conservative Joiners

% naming each issue as a priority for...

Britain as a whole

	Issue	%
	Brexit	72%
	Immigration	56%
	NHS	40%
	Economy and jobs	30%

Me and my family

	Issue	%
	Brexit	53%
	NHS	48%
	Immigration	40%
	Cost of living	33%

Conservative party

	Issue	%
	Brexit	77%
	Immigration	42%
	NHS	29%
	Economy and jobs	27%

Labour party

	Issue	%
	NHS	36%
	Social care	23%
	Tackling poverty	21%
	Brexit	17%

Lord Ashcroft Polls
@LordAshcroft

Most Joiners say they think the Conservative Party is competent and capable. They are also more likely to agree than disagree (and much more likely than voters as a whole to agree) that the party shares their values, wants to help ordinary people get on in life, is on the side of people like themselves, and stands for fairness and opportunity for all.

Joiners are much more likely than voters in general (but less so than Conservative Loyalists) to believe that a person who works hard can be successful in Britain whatever their background. Like most voters, a small majority say they think life in Britain today is better than it was thirty years ago – making them somewhat less positive on this question than Conservative Loyalists. Joiners are less likely than Tories in general, and much less likely than the population as a whole, to think of multiculturalism, social liberalism, feminism, the green movement, globalisation and immigration as forces for good.

It was clear from our post-election focus groups that those who switched to the Conservatives had been no more delighted about an early election than anyone else ("I felt disheartened and angry;" "a waste of time and money, and where has it got us?"). Nor were they particularly impressed by the Tory campaign ("a bit of a shambles"), or many of the party's policy proposals (and "clearly Theresa May wasn't convinced they were the right thing as they binned quite a few during the campaign").

One thing that united our participants was that they were not convinced by Labour in general or its leader in particular: "I have voted Labour all my adult life but would not vote for Jeremy Corbyn. He is divisive and his promises are empty." Some liked his ideas but thought them wildly unrealistic: "The overall Labour message was based on giving things out for free;" "It was almost as if they knew they would lose, so they promised what they liked." Others said they could not imagine Corbyn "being a world leader and trying to discuss our future with the likes of Putin and Trump", or even believed him "a huge threat to the security of our country". Many said they had voted "through gritted teeth" and had been put off by Labour, not inspired by their principal opponents: "The Conservatives are the losers in an ugly baby contest."

"It felt as though we had to choose between Brexit and improvements to things that affect us on an everyday basis, like healthcare and education... With Brexit being a once-in-a-lifetime chance, it was simply too important not to swing my vote."

Another, unsurprisingly, was Brexit. For most of these people, Britain's EU departure was the pre-eminent issue of the day, whether they liked it or not (and most of them did), and that meant choosing the party and leader best placed to handle it. Many thought the Conservatives were "the only party to go with if you wanted to see Brexit followed through. Other parties just don't seem to have the stomach for it." Labour's "meandering position was just too confusing", and several believed that apart from the Tories, "no other party really wants it". That is not to say that they all found the decision easy: "I did feel somewhat helpless, as it felt as though we had to choose between Brexit and improvements to things that affect us on an everyday basis, like healthcare and education. These things are incredibly important, but with Brexit being a once-in-a-lifetime chance, it was simply too important not to swing my vote."

"Someone said to me recently 'I know you voted Tory' as if I had killed someone."

Inevitably, this meant they were voting Conservative simply as the least bad alternative or to get a job done. Some said this had been "quite a big deal" for them ("I thought I might get struck by lightning;" "my grandad would be gobsmacked if he were still alive, as he always told me never to trust a Tory;" "Someone said to me recently 'I know you voted Tory' as if I had killed someone"). This meant most did not feel any deeper affinity with the party: "Personally, working in education, I had to put my work life aside for this vote as I don't feel they stand for much of what I believe in, but they were in very much the best position to guide us through the next few years;" "The Conservatives remain too heavily reliant on the grey vote and large corporate interests. That said, they seem likely to keep the plates spinning for longer before we slump into the next recession;" "I voted Conservative mainly to protect Brexit. Other than that, I don't agree with their ethics;" "I am a younger voter and voted Conservative but I don't feel particularly 'liked' by the party, or as if they had my best interests at heart."

In fact, although they had still thought the Tories a less unpalatable option than Labour, few now thought better of the party or Theresa May than they had done previously: "I believed they were going in the right direction in trying to get people from my background to support them, but the recent election put that idea to bed;" "I am not too sure that Mrs. May is a strong PM. She seemed to get a bit flustered over the past few months and looks like she needs a good night's sleep. I would really like to see her as strong as she was when she took over the party;" "She is a control freak who lost control."

This in turn meant that they did not now consider themselves to be "Conservative voters". Several said their decision had been "tactical" or that they had been "lending" their vote because of the circumstances: "My heart isn't with the Conservative Party." Most said they would stick with the Tories if another election were to arrive very soon ("Voting any other way at this stage feels like a big risk that I don't know that I'd be willing to take, despite the advantages of policies offered by other parties that could directly benefit me"), but beyond that they could see themselves going in different directions: "I would like to vote for Labour next time round but not until they have another leader."

Meanwhile, people felt unsettled about events and what lay in store: "An outside observer would wonder what sort of brilliant tragi-comedy they were watching. 'You couldn't make this s*** up'." The government was "weaker" than it had been, and preoccupied with "questions over succession planning and leadership challenges", though the country was in "stormy waters" and needed "a strong government to see us through".

Conservative Considerers

Considerers said at some point during the campaign that they intended to vote Conservative, but did not ultimately do so. Of those who turned out, six in ten voted Labour, but more than half did not vote. Only 38 per cent said they always voted at general elections.

The Considerers' median age is 49. Their geographical distribution, spread of social grades, level of education, and their likelihood of working and having children at home is similar to that of the population as a whole. On the political scale they put themselves to the right of Defectors and well to the right of the electorate in general, but to the left of Conservative Joiners.

Having thought about voting Conservative in 2017, one in five say they were deterred by the policies the party announced during the campaign. Nearly as many were put off by the way the Tories came across overall during the election (the single biggest reason for Considerers who had voted stay in the EU). The remaining three most common reasons were that the Tories had not focused on the issues they cared about; that they were put off by Theresa May as leader, and that they did not think the Conservative Party was on their side. More than one in five Considerers who voted Labour say they were attracted away from the Tories by another party's policies, and a similar proportion that they decided another party was more on the side of people like them.

Only one in twenty say they would choose a different party if they could go back to the 2017 election and vote again, and three quarters of that group would vote Conservative – but those who voted Labour are much happier with their decision than other Considerers. Nearly half of all Considerers say their view of the Tories has become less favourable since the election; only 12 per cent say it has become more positive.

In the referendum, Considerers voted to leave the EU by a much bigger margin than the country as a whole, but they were less likely to turn out than Conservative Loyalists, Joiners or Defectors. Though more than half support Brexit, they are twice as likely as Loyalists and nearly four times as likely as Joiners to say they would like to prevent it from happening.

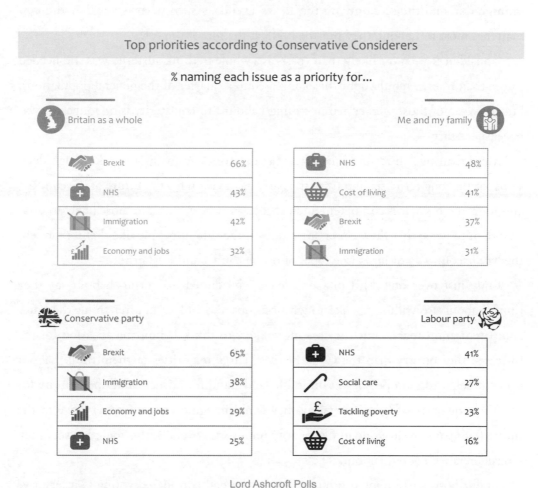

Top priorities according to Conservative Considerers

% naming each issue as a priority for...

Britain as a whole

	Brexit	66%
	NHS	43%
	Immigration	42%
	Economy and jobs	32%

Me and my family

	NHS	48%
	Cost of living	41%
	Brexit	37%
	Immigration	31%

Conservative party

	Brexit	65%
	Immigration	38%
	Economy and jobs	29%
	NHS	25%

Labour party

	NHS	41%
	Social care	27%
	Tackling poverty	23%
	Cost of living	16%

Lord Ashcroft Polls
@LordAshcroft

While Considerers name Brexit as the most important issue facing Britain as a whole, they rank it third – behind improving the NHS and tackling the cost of living – when asked what matters to themselves and their families. Only one in four say they think the NHS is a high priority for the Conservative Party, ranking it behind Brexit, immigration and the economy on the Tories' agenda. Asked what issues they thought mattered most to Labour, they put the NHS at the top of the list.

Considerers are more likely than voters as a whole to think austerity was still needed (more than four in ten thought this, compared to a quarter of the general population), but six in ten of those who ended up voting Labour think austerity is no longer, or was never, necessary.

More than two thirds of Considerers say the Tories are willing to take tough decisions for the long term, six in ten say the party has a vision for the future of the country, and four in ten say it is competent and capable. However, they are more likely to disagree than to agree that the Conservatives are on the side of people like them, represent the whole country not just some types of people, and stand for fairness.

Only just over one third of Considerers who ended up voting Labour say they think Labour are willing to take tough decisions and only a quarter think the party competent and capable, but they are more likely to think Labour has a vision for the future of the country than the Conservatives. Large majorities of them think Labour want to help ordinary people get on in life, and stand for fairness and opportunity for all. Three quarters of Considerers say they could imagine voting Conservative in the future (compared to just one in five of 2017 non-Tories overall); this included six in ten Considerers who voted Labour.

In our post-election focus groups, people who had considered voting Conservative but decided against it said they had initially been attracted to the party for several different reasons. Brexit was one of these, but so were the Labour leadership ("at first I would have voted Sooty and Sweep rather than Corbyn"), a more sensible approach to the economy ("however much I dislike them I think maybe when they seem harsh they are being more realistic financially than Corbyn, who is promising everything"), and their view of the Prime Minister: "I considered voting Tory because Mrs. May, at the start, came across as honest and refreshing. She soon changed, though."

"I wanted to give them a chance and kept waiting to hear something worthy of my vote, but it never came."

Equally, a number of different things had put them off. One was that, having called the election seeking a mandate for her negotiations with the EU, the PM seemed unable or unwilling to give any details of what she would be trying to negotiate: "the Brexit implications were skirted around;" "there was no plan or solution, just that the Conservatives would be strong and stable. There was no detail or real choice." To some, this suggested that the Tories were taking them, and the election, for granted – a view which seemed to be confirmed by the manner of the party's campaign: "they came across as cocky and as though it wasn't worth fighting for our votes. I would have voted Tory if May had turned up to the debates;" "if she had only bothered to actively take part and act like she genuinely cared for the country then I would have voted for her;" "She seemed afraid to stand up to scrutiny;" "I wanted to give them a chance and kept waiting to hear something worthy of my vote, but it never came."

"I always did believe in economics and not spending what you don't have, but I'm fed up with being shafted so I voted Labour."

Some were actively put off by various Conservative manifesto pledges, especially those affecting pensioners: "I nearly voted Tory until that daft thing about crucifying the OAPs. I'm a natural Tory voter and it was only her targeting pensioners that put me off;" "I always did believe in economics and not spending what you don't have, but I'm fed up with being shafted so I voted Labour;" "Completely out of touch. Fox hunting and grammar schools? I don't know anyone who wants to hear that;" "Just as I was about to vote Tory for the first time in decades, they ruined it all with the triple lock and the return of fox hunting. They might as well have announced the legalisation of hunting pensioners with hounds." The party's programme felt "negative, austere, nothing to give a sense of optimism;" "They thought they could offer little and get a big reward."

Conservative Defectors

Defectors voted Conservative at the 2015 general election but did not do so in June 2017. More than one third of them did not vote at all; of those who turned out, six in ten went to Labour and three went to the Liberal Democrats. Just under three quarters say they are happy with their decision; less than two in a hundred say they would choose the Conservatives if they had the chance to go back and vote again.

The median age of Defectors is 45 – younger than Conservative Loyalists, Joiners and Considerers. They are three times as likely as Loyalists and twice as likely as Joiners to be aged 34 or under, and they are considerably more likely than Joiners to be in the AB and C1 social groups. Defectors are more likely than the population as a whole and (especially) Joiners to have a degree or to live in London or the South East. They are more likely than both Conservative voters and the electorate in general to be working, to have children at home, and to have a mortgage. Though Defectors are more likely to say they are slightly to the right of centre than to the left, they put themselves closer to the middle of the political scale than Conservative Loyalists or Joiners.

Nearly six in ten Defectors who turned out at the referendum voted to remain in the EU. Remainers who had voted Tory in 2015 divided in two important ways. First, by age: 44 per cent of those aged under 50 defected, compared to less than a quarter of those aged 50 and over. Second, by their attitude to Brexit: only just over one in five who accept Britain's EU departure switched away from the Tories, compared to more than half of those who say they would still like to prevent Brexit from happening. Conservative Defectors are more likely than voters as a whole – and four times as likely as those who voted Conservative – to say they want to stop Brexit going ahead.

How a member of this group voted in the EU referendum also had an important bearing on the manner of their defection from the Tories. Among remainers who voted Conservative in 2015 but not in 2017, 46 per cent went to Labour and a further three in ten to the Lib Dems; only 19 per cent did not vote. Among leavers who defected from the Tories, 46 per cent stayed at home; only just over one in three went to Labour and less than one in ten to the Lib Dems.

Negotiating Britain's EU departure on the right terms is all but tied with improving the NHS among Defectors' most important priorities for the country, but the NHS is top, followed by the cost of living, in the list of issues that matter to themselves and their families. They see Brexit as the Conservative Party's clear priority, followed by immigration, the deficit and the economy. Defectors are nearly two and a half times as likely to say that improving the NHS is important to them as to say they believe it a priority for the Conservative Party (but almost as likely to say it is a priority for Labour as to say it matters to them). Less than three in ten Defectors think austerity should continue; the majority think no more cuts are needed, or that austerity was always unnecessary and was just an excuse to cut public services.

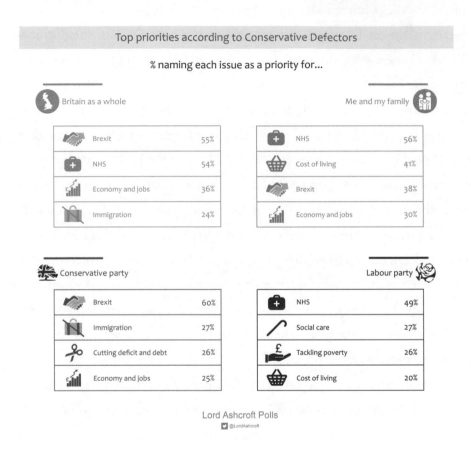

Top priorities according to Conservative Defectors

% naming each issue as a priority for...

Britain as a whole

Brexit	55%
NHS	54%
Economy and jobs	36%
Immigration	24%

Me and my family

NHS	56%
Cost of living	41%
Brexit	38%
Economy and jobs	30%

Conservative party

Brexit	60%
Immigration	27%
Cutting deficit and debt	26%
Economy and jobs	25%

Labour party

NHS	49%
Social care	27%
Tackling poverty	26%
Cost of living	20%

Lord Ashcroft Polls
@LordAshcroft

Most Defectors say they think the Tories are willing to take tough decisions for the long term and just under half say the party has a vision for the future of the country. However, less than a quarter think the Conservatives are competent and capable (compared to more than six in ten of those who voted Tory) or want to help ordinary people get on in life, and fewer than one in five say they think the party is on the side of people like them, shares their values or stands for fairness. Only one in five Defectors think Labour shares what they see as the Tories' chief virtue of being willing to take tough decisions, but they are as likely to think Labour has a vision for the country as to think this true of the Conservatives. Two thirds believe Labour want to help ordinary people get on in life, and most think the party's heart is in the right place. Two thirds of Defectors who did not turn out in 2017 say they could imagine voting Conservative again in the future; among those who ended up switching to a different party, only just over half say they could see themselves going back to the Tories.

Defectors are more likely than the population as a whole (but less likely than Conservative voters) to think it possible for a hard-working person to succeed in Britain whatever their background, and that life in Britain today is better overall than it was thirty years ago. They are more likely than voters in general (and much more likely than those who had voted Conservative) to think multiculturalism, social liberalism, feminism, the green movement, globalisation and immigration are forces for good.

Asked in our post-election focus groups why they had voted Conservative in 2015, Defectors usually offered two sets of reasons: that the Tories were doing reasonably well in government, particularly on the economy, and that they were happy with David Cameron, at least in contrast to Ed Miliband. The Conservatives were "doing a good job with credible leaders getting the country out of the enormous pickle that the Labour Party had got us into". Cameron "was a good leader I trusted", was "strong and got stuff done" and had "a ton of confidence", while "Miliband was clearly useless", and his party not ready to govern.

"We're getting tired of politics, thank you very much, so if you want us to vote again you're going to have to be nice and convincing."

Though most did not like the idea of an early election ("there was an arrogance about it") some said they had intended to vote Tory at the start of the campaign. But because the Tories "thought they would walk it", they misjudged the mood: "We're getting tired of politics, thank you very much, so if you want us to vote again you're going to have to be nice and convincing." In the event, they were "a bit half-hearted until it was too late".

"She only seemed to care about Brexit and not the things that, right now, are more important to me. I didn't feel they were interested in me and people like me, so they lost my vote."

Some even agreed that Brexit was the issue of the day, but took a very different view of the subject from Theresa May: "I don't want Brexit, but if it's going to happen I wanted other parties to be consulted. I'd like to think a cross-party Brexit could happen;" "I wanted to refuse her a mandate;" "I didn't like how they essentially just adopted all the UKIP values." More often, the problem was that the Conservatives "focused so much on Brexit policy that they completely forgot to campaign on other things. I think they thought that people cared more about Brexit than social care and health, pensions and so on. Big mistake;" "She only seemed to care about Brexit and not the things that, right now, are more important to me. I didn't feel they were interested in me and people like me, so they lost my vote."

Specific issues had also played a part in their decision not to stick with the Tories, including the "Dementia Tax" social care policy, the NHS, changes to pension entitlements and, for several participants, the prospect of a free vote in parliament to lift the ban on fox hunting: "Although it's not a seismic issue, I could never vote for the return of fox hunting. Once society starts backtracking we might start losing the ground we have gained on equality, LGBTQ, race, capital punishment. Forwards please, not backwards."

Labour, meanwhile, seemed "positive not just in its politics, but in its solutions. In contrast, the Conservatives' proposed solutions were very negative," and Jeremy Corbyn was more convincing than many had expected: "I actually started to believe in Labour policies." Some were candid in declaring their self-interest: "I wanted the tuition free-bie." Not everyone was impressed by Labour "promising the old tax and spend routine that us older people have seen fail before", but the combined effect – "the negative drip of arrogance and U-turns, with Labour making all the ground" – was enough to rule out a Conservative vote.

Few in these groups ruled out voting Tory again at the next election, but none now considered themselves loyal to any one party ("I guess I am floating now"). It was clear, though, that they had less confidence in the Conservative Party now than was the case when the election was called, let alone when they voted Tory in 2015. Though some thought it was good that Theresa May had been "brought down a few pegs", the government seemed weakened at a crucial time in international negotiations, and were "busy fighting among themselves". The Tories "seem to be overwhelmed by Brexit. Theresa May started out well but hasn't had the staying power that David Cameron had;" "People need a strong leader, even if they're telling you a load of crap." Instead, Britain now had "a bit of a lame dog PM". This left some feeling more nervous about the future, especially over Brexit ("it fills me with dread"), but none of these Defectors were eager for another election any time soon: "I'm sick to the back teeth of it all."

* * *

This final sentiment eloquently sums up how much of the country currently feels about electoral politics. Most have had quite enough excitement for now; the idea of calm, sensible government has never sounded so appealing. For the Conservatives, this is just as well: going back up against a confident and energised Labour Party in the short term is hardly something they would relish.

But they will have to do so sooner or later, and that means assembling a coalition of voters to keep it in office. In 2017, the Tories won an extra 5.5 per cent of the vote compared to two years earlier, and 2.3 million more ballots were cast in their favour. But as we have seen, the party's vote had changed as well as grown. Those leaving the Conservative voting coalition were younger, more highly educated, more "white collar", more socially liberal and less enthusiastic about Brexit and continued austerity than those who stayed or joined.

Meanwhile, the most significant shift in the Labour vote, which grew by 9.5 per cent, or 3.5 million – is that it became younger. This brings its own challenge for the next contest: stoking the enthusiasm of people who do not usually bother with elections but were inspired to do so by Jeremy Corbyn and his manifesto, while setting out a programme for government that people who did not turn out for them this time will find responsible and realistic as well as uplifting.

At the same time, the Conservatives in government must deal with the colossal challenges of the coming years in a way that restores their reputation for competence, wins the confidence of those who fear the country is heading the wrong way, holds the allegiance of those who supported them for the first time, and brings back the kinds of voters who decided in 2017 that the party was not for them. Politics was never meant to be easy.

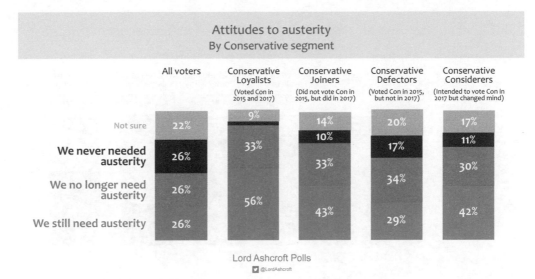

Attitudes to austerity
By Conservative segment

	All voters	Conservative Loyalists (Voted Con in 2015 and 2017)	Conservative Joiners (Did not vote Con in 2015, but did in 2017)	Conservative Defectors (Voted Con in 2015, but not in 2017)	Conservative Considerers (Intended to vote Con in 2017 but changed mind)
Not sure	22%	9%	14%	20%	17%
We never needed austerity	26%	33%	10%	17%	11%
We no longer need austerity	26%	56%	33%	34%	30%
We still need austerity	26%		43%	29%	42%

Lord Ashcroft Polls
@LordAshcroft

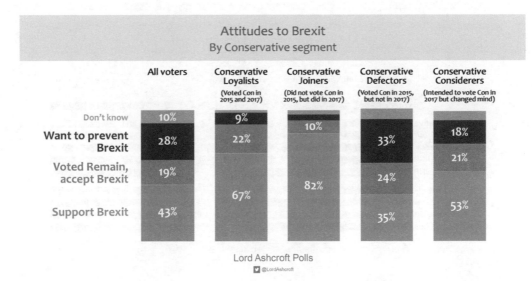

Attitudes to Brexit
By Conservative segment

	All voters	Conservative Loyalists (Voted Con in 2015 and 2017)	Conservative Joiners (Did not vote Con in 2015, but did in 2017)	Conservative Defectors (Voted Con in 2015, but not in 2017)	Conservative Considerers (Intended to vote Con in 2017 but changed mind)
Don't know	10%	9%	10%	33%	18%
Want to prevent Brexit	28%	22%			21%
Voted Remain, accept Brexit	19%	67%	82%	24%	
Support Brexit	43%			35%	53%

Lord Ashcroft Polls
@LordAshcroft

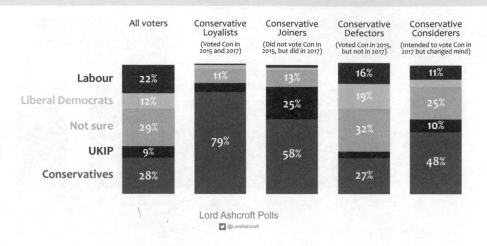

Best party to handle Brexit
By Conservative segment

Lord Ashcroft Polls
@LordAshcroft

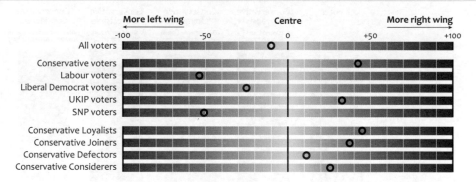

2017 voters on the left-right spectrum

Lord Ashcroft Polls
@LordAshcroft

Below are some pairs of statements. Please say which statement in each pair you most agree with, even if you don't completely agree with it

If you work hard, it is possible to be very successful in Britain no matter what your background

In Britain today, people from some backgrounds will never have a real chance to be successful no matter how hard they work

	Agree 1	Agree 2
All voters	54%	46%
Labour voters	33%	67%
Conservative Loyalists	87%	13%
Conservative Joiners	72%	28%
Conservative Defectors	63%	37%
Conservative Considerers	68%	32%

50%

For most children growing up in Britain today, life will be better than it was for their parents

For most children growing up in Britain today, life will be worse than it was for their parents

	Agree 1	Agree 2
All voters	40%	60%
Labour voters	28%	72%
Conservative Loyalists	59%	41%
Conservative Joiners	49%	51%
Conservative Defectors	40%	60%
Conservative Considerers	43%	57%

50%

People have a right to things like decent housing, healthcare, education and enough to live on, and the government should make sure everyone has them

People are too ready to talk about their rights – people have a responsibility to provide for themselves and should not expect the government to do so for them

	Agree 1	Agree 2
All voters	55%	45%
Labour voters	81%	19%
Conservative Loyalists	22%	78%
Conservative Joiners	33%	67%
Conservative Defectors	46%	54%
Conservative Considerers	44%	56%

50%

Overall, life in Britain today is better than it was 30 years ago

Overall, life in Britain today is worse than it was 30 years ago

	Agree 1	Agree 2
All voters	52%	48%
Labour voters	46%	54%
Conservative Loyalists	71%	29%
Conservative Joiners	56%	44%
Conservative Defectors	58%	42%
Conservative Considerers	55%	45%

50%

Lord Ashcroft Polls
@LordAshcroft

	CONSERVATIVE LOYALISTS	CONSERVATIVE JOINERS	CONSERVATIVE DEFECTORS	CONSERVATIVE CONSIDERERS
	Voted Conservative in 2015 and 2017	Did not vote Conservative in 2015, but did in 2017	Voted Conservative in 2015, but not in 2017	Intended to vote Conservative in 2017 but changed mind
Median age	61	56	45	49
Class and education	More AB, fewer graduates than general population	More C2DE, fewer graduates than the general population and Conservative Loyalists	More ABC1, more graduates than the general population	Similar social grade and education levels to the general population
Family	61% are married 16% have children at home	53% are married 18% have children at home	48% are married 24% have children at home	51% are married 24% have children at home
Employment	34% work full time 44% are retired	34% work full time 34% are retired	48% work full time 21% are retired	40% work full time 25% are retired
Home ownership	82% own their home, 54% outright	68% own their home, 41% outright	65% own their home, 32% outright	64% own their home, 30% outright
Electoral traits	85% 'always vote' at general elections	45% voted UKIP in 2015, 14% for Labour, 8% Lib Dems	38% voted Labour in 2017, 19% Lib Dems. 36% didn't vote	25% voted Labour in 2017, 8% Lib Dems. 59% didn't vote
		68% 'always vote' at general elections	57% 'always vote' at general elections	38% 'always vote' at general elections
EU referendum vote	Leave 64% / 32% Remain	Leave 75% / 13% Remain	Leave 35% / 50% Remain	Leave 49% / 23% Remain
View on Brexit	Support 67% / Accept 22% / Oppose 9%	Support 82% / Accept 10% / Oppose 5	Support 35% / Accept 24% / Oppose 33%	Support 53% / Accept 21% / Oppose 18%
Best party on Brexit	79% CON	58% CON / 25% UKIP	27% CON / 35% LAB/LD / 32% UNSURE	48% CON / 25% UNSURE

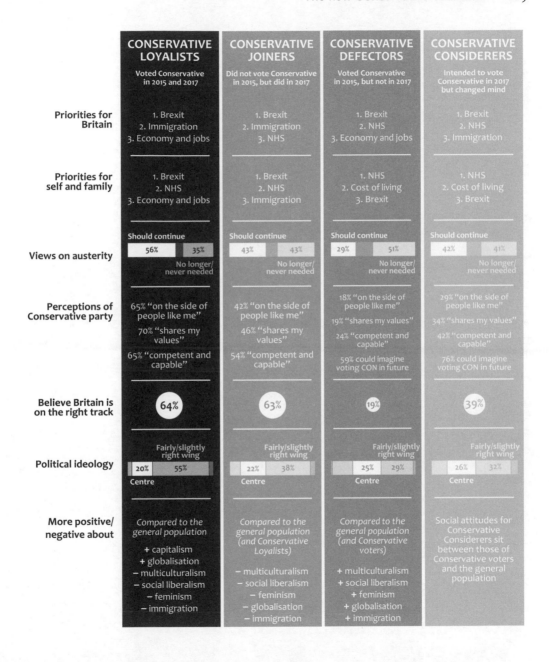

	CONSERVATIVE LOYALISTS	CONSERVATIVE JOINERS	CONSERVATIVE DEFECTORS	CONSERVATIVE CONSIDERERS
	Voted Conservative in 2015 and 2017	Did not vote Conservative in 2015, but did in 2017	Voted Conservative in 2015, but not in 2017	Intended to vote Conservative in 2017 but changed mind
Priorities for Britain	1. Brexit 2. Immigration 3. Economy and jobs	1. Brexit 2. Immigration 3. NHS	1. Brexit 2. NHS 3. Economy and jobs	1. Brexit 2. NHS 3. Immigration
Priorities for self and family	1. Brexit 2. NHS 3. Economy and jobs	1. Brexit 2. NHS 3. Immigration	1. NHS 2. Cost of living 3. Brexit	1. NHS 2. Cost of living 3. Brexit
Views on austerity	Should continue 56% / 35% No longer/never needed	Should continue 43% / 43% No longer/never needed	Should continue 29% / 51% No longer/never needed	Should continue 42% / 41% No longer/never needed
Perceptions of Conservative party	65% "on the side of people like me" 70% "shares my values" 65% "competent and capable"	42% "on the side of people like me" 46% "shares my values" 54% "competent and capable"	18% "on the side of people like me" 19% "shares my values" 24% "competent and capable" 59% could imagine voting CON in future	29% "on the side of people like me" 34% "shares my values" 42% "competent and capable" 76% could imagine voting CON in future
Believe Britain is on the right track	64%	63%	19%	39%
Political ideology	Fairly/slightly right wing 20% / 55% Centre	Fairly/slightly right wing 22% / 38% Centre	Fairly/slightly right wing 25% / 29% Centre	Fairly/slightly right wing 26% / 32% Centre
More positive/ negative about	Compared to the general population + capitalism + globalisation − multiculturalism − social liberalism − feminism − immigration	Compared to the general population (and Conservative Loyalists) − multiculturalism − social liberalism − feminism − globalisation − immigration	Compared to the general population (and Conservative voters) + multiculturalism + social liberalism + feminism + globalisation + immigration	Social attitudes for Conservative Considerers sit between those of Conservative voters and the general population

Methodological note

26 focus groups with undecided voters were held throughout Great Britain between 2nd May and 1st June 2017.

14,384 people who had voted in person, by proxy or by post were interviewed by telephone or online between 6th and 8th June 2017.

20,557 adults were interviewed online between 29th June and 13th July 2017. Results were weighted to be representative of all adults in Great Britain.

10 focus groups were held between 18th and 26th July 2017 comprising first-time voters; people who voted leave in the EU referendum or UKIP in the 2015 general election and Labour in 2017; people who considered voting Conservative in 2017 but decided not to; people who voted Conservative in 2015 but not in 2017; and people who did not vote Conservative in 2015 but did in 2017.

Full data tables for the polls can be found at LordAshcroftPolls.com